How To Bluff Your Way To Independence

Edited by

Brian Monteith

Greenmantle

Greenmantle

ISBN 978-0-9567579-5-1

Printed in Great Britain by
Berforts Information Press Ltd
King's Lynn
Norfolk PE31 6AG

Typeset by Andrew Hook

Published by:
Greenmantle Publishing
1/5 Dickson Place
Cross Road
Peebles EH45 8LA

greenmantlepublishing@gmail.com

Contents

Introduction

On Thursday 18th September Scotland faces its biggest ever democratic decision. Those able to vote – and it is not all Scots that would normally be entitled to vote in Scottish constituencies that are being allowed to – will be able to choose if Scotland should remain as part of the United Kingdom of Great Britain and Northern Ireland, or if it should start afresh as a sovereign nation.

Never before has Scotland's people been given a direct say in such a momentous life-altering and future-shaping decision. When the Scottish and English Parliaments decided to unite under the Acts of Union back in 1707 neither institutions were what we would now describe as democratic. Since that time British democracy has evolved to the point where universal suffrage was achieved and adults were able to elect Members of Parliament – and latterly members of the Scottish Parliament – but at no time has the Scottish public elected a majority of Scottish Nationalist MPs to Westminster on a mandate to either hold a referendum or negotiate Scotland's repudiation of the Union.

The Scottish people seemed content with the Union. General Elections were contested on wider issues with the question of independence never determining the Scottish vote – although electing SNP members in the 1970s did contribute to the formation and fall of Labour governments – ironically, ushering in Margaret Thatcher's premiership as a result.

The Scottish Parliament elections of 2011 changed all that. Although independence is the SNP's core belief it had not been the core message of the SNP campaign, but the party's unprecedented absolute majority in a proportional voting system made it politically impossible for it to avoid holding a referendum on the independence question. Bounced into such a commitment by Alex Salmond's comments during a BBC radio interview, nationalists were nonetheless ecstatic that at last the question of Scotland's membership of the UK would now be tested. Taken aback by the scale of the SNP victory only a year after Scotland had voted for Labour in greater force than it had in 2005, the unionist parties were caught off guard.

Finally, after much shadow boxing by both unionists and nationalists an agreement was reached about the conduct of the referendum that Prime Minister David Cameron and First Minister Alex Salmond could sign up to. With the 'Edinburgh Agreement' settled, the process began.

Since then much has been made of the unionist's inability to provide an alternative view to independence that might be presented as a positive case for the Union. Critics allege this is due to the inability of the three main unionist parties that have formed the Better Together campaign to offer a new constitutional settlement. This criticism is wholly unfounded and wrong.

It is wrong in principle because there is a positive case for the Union irrespective of the likelihood or desirability of any further constitutional change.

It is also wrong in practice because even though the case for the existing Union – in terms of economy, social solidarity, security, welfare and more – are advantageous to Scotland the Union is evolving as we live and breath.

Put simply – in this world where nations gather together to share risk and opportunity, where sovereignty is regularly sacrificed by pooling it with others and, as a result, being occasionally in a minority is considered a price worth paying for accessing mutual benefits – if Scotland was not in the United Kingdom already it would be seeking to join.

Furthermore, the application of the Scotland Act 2012 will bring additional devolution not yet experienced – and all three main unionist parties are signed up to extending the powers and responsibilities of the Scottish Parliament further. That the Scotland Act 2012 was delivered in the teeth of nationalist opposition gives great weight to the credibility of unionist commitments to go further still.

Devolution across the UK – in Wales and Northern Ireland too – is the growing trend. Localism is happening, even though the SNP seeks to use Holyrood's authority to centralise more and more state control in Edinburgh.

By contrast, the SNP has sought to denigrate the Westminster Parliament at every turn, blame it for every woe, and cultivate grievances where none have previously existed. The Prime Minster is challenged to a public debate, but as soon as he crosses the border he is attacked by the same people for having the temerity to open his mouth. It is suggested the government and its Ministers – such as George Osborne – have no mandate, and yet the Coalition Government parties attracted more votes in Scotland than the SNP in the General Election of 2010.

The nationalists' attacks on the United Kingdom, its institutions, its politicians (especially its politicians) and what it stands for cannot be described as anything other than negative. Typical of this approach is to claim that only an independent Scotland can protect the NHS – when health is a devolved responsibility and Scotland already chooses to spend significantly more of its government funding on the NHS than the rest of the UK.

While this negativity has been intentionally fomenting discontent the SNP government has used hundreds of thousands of pounds of taxpayers money to issue a White Paper (with accompanying fanfare and roadshow) that purports to show how it would shape an independent Scotland and give reassurance about what will happen if Scots decide to leave the UK. It is nothing other than a partisan political manifesto that needs to be challenged as the grand bluff that it is.

It is in response to this bluff that this book is published.

Gathered together here are a selection of articles written by contributors to the political website ThinkScotland.org from the time of the launch of the White Paper into Spring this year. It is not a page by page or para by para dissection, instead it charts the initial reaction and then the unfolding astonishment as more and more of what is claimed in the White Paper is analysed and shown wanting.

This will, to some, be said to be a negative exercise – but that is like saying challenging Mao's Little Red Book, or any other party manifesto, is negative when such a process reveals the deliberate obfuscation, the selective use of statistics and the sheer nonsense on stilts contained in such a publication.

Challenging the bluff and bluster of politicians is a positive public service and this book seeks to do that.

So when, for example, Neil Craig maps out how the SNP's childcare proposals are based upon economic invention, when Murdo Fraser and Bill Jamieson take us through the contradictions and consequences of the SNP's currency proposals, or when Ben Acheson and Jonathan Stanley reveal the holes in the case about Scottish EU membership they are writing positively in seeking to defend Scotland's interests.

There is an honourable case for Scottish independence – but it is not in the White Paper. By seeking to suggest that Scotland will enjoy nothing but unadulterated peace and happiness, that there are no risks, no downsides to independence – and that we shall have nothing but munificent and beneficial relations with the rest of the UK following a velvet divorce – the SNP Government and its White Paper is seeking to bluff the voters into believing the impossible.

There are risks, those risks are real for many peoples' livelihoods – and in considering the future hopes and aspirations of their children and generations beyond them the risks become exponential.

Presenting a wholly positive case for the Union requires not just a statement of what is possible and desirable by being a member of the United Kingdom – and I know this project to already be in hand – it also requires the searing white heat of daylight being brought upon government claims and assertions that cannot be substantiated and are often invented.

That is what this book seeks to do. You may not agree with what every contributor says, indeed I would be surprised if that is possible – for they write from such a wide variety of outlooks – but it should surely make you think about the benefits already inherent in being a member of the UK and ask why would we leave that association only to then try and obtain so much of what we already have.

Brian Monteith
May 2014

About the authors...

BEN ACHESON
Born and raised in Ballynahinch, Northern Ireland, Ben Acheson works as a
Policy Adviser at the European Parliament in Brussels. Graduating with a First
in geography at Northumbria University, Ben then gained an M.Litt in Peace
and Conflict Studies from the University of St Andrews. Ben is the presenter
of the current affairs web-series entitled 'A Different Angle' and in his spare
time he plays semi-professional American Football, being named Belgian
Player of the Year 2012 and 2013.

HUGH ANDREW
A Paisley buddy, Hugh Andrew was educated in Glasgow and fled to
Magdalen College, Oxford, to study history. He started in the book business
with James Thin Ltd; after running the Paisley branch of Hatchards he set up
his own business and was for a period joint Managing Director of Canongate.
Hugh established Birlinn in 1992 and it is now one of Scotland's largest
publishers. He is Chairman of the Tuesday Club.

JAMES CORBETT
James Corbett writes with a dry wit for various on-line publications, but is also
seeking new opportunities to deploy his multifarious talents (looking for work,
to you and me, Ed). In his spare time he enjoys boat building, coastal rowing
and cars. He lives in Troon, but on the up-side doesn't play golf and has never
owned a v-neck sweater.

NEIL CRAIG
A member of UKIP – after he was expelled from the Liberal Democrats on the
grounds that speaking in favour of economic liberalism is officially
"incompatible with party membership"! Neil runs a science fiction bookshop in
Glasgow and his pro-technology and free market blog *A Place To Stand*. Neil
has been contributing to ThinkScotland.org for the last four years.

MURDO FRASER MSP
Born and educated in Inverness, Murdo graduated from Aberdeen University
in 1986 with a postgraduate Diploma in Legal Studies and practiced in
Commercial law before becoming an MSP in 2001. Murdo was Deputy Leader
of the Scottish Conservatives from 2005 to 2011 and is now spokesman for
Enterprise, Energy and Tourism as well as Convener of the Parliament's
Economy, Energy and Tourism Committee.

BILL JAMIESON

A former Business Journalist of the Year, in 2012 Bill Jamieson was accorded a Lifetime Achievement Award by the Scottish Newspaper Society. Born in Ayrshire and now living in Edinburgh, Bill has specialised in financial journalism and economics for over forty years. He recently stepped down as Executive Editor of The Scotsman and has now launched Scot-Buzz, a website supporting enterprise and business start-ups.

ROBERT KILGOUR

A serial entrepreneur, investor and property developer Robert was the original founder of Four Seasons Health Care which is now the UK's largest care home operator with some 500 homes and over 30,000 staff. Born in Edinburgh, brought up in Fife, educated at Loretto, Robert currently divides his time between his home in Westminster, his cottage on the Fife coast and his main office in Musselburgh.

VIVIAN LINACRE

Two years younger than the Queen and David Attenborough, Vivian Linacre's pace of life is hotting up. Having published books on megalithic maths, customary weights and measures and Georgian Perth, he is finishing a history of the UK commercial property market 1950-75 that coincided with his early career. With only four sons, eight grandchildren and two great-grandchildren so far, the twenty-teens look full of promise, but for Scotland there is much to do.

DAVID MEIKLE

Glasgow born and bred, David Meikle is the only Conservative councillor in the city, earning him the nickname "David the Tory". A Glasgow University politics graduate, he lives in Shawlands with his SNP activist girlfriend. Although politics has always been an obsession David has also worked in customer service, audit and consultancy. He enjoys gin, classical music and eating.

BRIAN MONTEITH

A Porty High School FP, Brian was infected by the bug of student politics when he studied architecture at Edinburgh College of Art in the mid-70s, becoming chairman of the UK Conservative Students and later chairman of the Scottish 'Young" Conservatives. After practicing public relations in London and Edinburgh throughout the 80s and 90s he served eight years in the Scottish Parliament before returning to commerce, working in Africa, Asia and the Caribbean. He is a regular columnist in *The Scotsman & Evening News* and is Editor of ThinkScotland.org and TheFreeSoceity.org

ANDREW MORRISON

Andrew Morrison is a Fellow of the Association of Chartered Certified Accountants and approved Scottish Conservative candidate for the 2015 General Election. Being born next to Ibrox Stadium, then moving to the Glasgow's East End in the shadows of Celtic Park, he now resides adjacent to Hampden Stadium, the nearest Scotland has came to a hat-trick for many a decade. Andrew appreciates orchestral music, the theatre, fast cars, and faster payment of fees.

DAVID PURDIE

Prof. David Purdie is a Doctor of Medicine and a Fellow of the Royal College of Physicians of Edinburgh. His central interest is in the scientific and literary components of The Enlightenment. Educated at Ayr Academy and Glasgow University, he was Postgraduate Dean of Hull University's Medical School and is now a Hon. Fellow of Edinburgh University's Institute for Advanced Studies in the Humanities. He is Editor-in-Chief of the Burns Encyclopaedia and of new editions of *Ivanhoe* and *Heart of Midlothian*. He is presently engaged on an edition of David Hume's philosophical assaults on religion.

PETER SMAILL

Based partly in London, Peter Smaill has been a private equity and venture capital specialist for over 30 years, involved in funding major Scottish management buy-outs and early stage high-tech investments. Since his career began he has advocated greater use of market solutions to ensure a better match between actual Scottish consumer preferences and allocation of national resources, currently dominated by assumptions of the superiority of state planning. He lives with his family when in Scotland at Borthwick, Midlothian, and also chairs the cultural charity Bach Network UK and writes programme notes for Bach and Handel concerts

IAN SMART

Ian Smart joined the Labour Party between the two 1974 General Elections. Despite everything he is still in it and plans only to resign in the unlikely eventuality that a Labour Government moves too far to the left, since he has been fully put the test in the other direction. He has a long association with the Party's Home Rule wing being a founder member of the Scottish Labour Action pressure group whose activities were critical to the Party's adoption of the Scottish Constitutional Convention scheme. A lawyer to trade he has for more than twenty years operated his own practice in Cumbernauld. Between 2008 and 2009 he was President of the Law Society of Scotland.

ALLAN SMITH

Born in Canada but living in Scotland since childhood, Allan Smith is a Law graduate & Independent Financial Adviser in Fife. He is also very active within politics and has stood for election as a candidate for the Scottish Conservative & Unionist Party on a number of occasions, most notably in the 2011 Scottish election. In his spare time Allan is a keen golfer and follower of cricket, in addition to being a long suffering supporter of Heart of Midlothian FC.

LIZ SMITH MSP

A former teacher at George Watsons' College and a political advisor to Sir Malcolm Rifkind, Liz Smith was elected to the Scottish Parliament in 2007 where she has held responsibility for the Conservatives for Education & Lifelong Learning and now Culture. & Sport. Capped several times for the Scottish Women's Cricket Team Liz lives at Madderty in South Perthshire.

JONATHAN STANLEY

The former Head of Policy and Treasurer for UKIP Scotland is currently working on health and young family related policy to further UKIP's appeal to women. Mr. Stanley is a member of the Royal College of Surgeons of England having previously studied Medicine and later Health Economics and Management at Sheffield University. He continues to study a PhD in Molecular Biology at Edinburgh University and remains in clinical practice.

IVOR TIEFENBRUN MBE

The founder of Linn Products in 1972 after he invented the seminal Sondek hi-fi turntable, Ivor Tiefenbrun was Scotland's Entrepreneur of the Year 2001 and received an MBE for services to the British industry. He is a visiting Professor of Strathclyde University's Department of Design Manufacture & Engineering Management and an Honorary Fellow of Glasgow School of Art. Ivor established the registered charity Cure Crohn's Colitis to fund IBD research.

EBEN WILSON

An Honours Graduate in Economics from St Andrews University Eben Wilson has had three careers in journalism (including Milton Friedman's TV series *Free to Choose*), economics (as an associate Scholar of the ASI) and business (founding various companies). Eben now concentrates on the development of Taxpayer Scotland, an independent voice on behalf of taxpayers that has emerged out of the national Taxpayers' Alliance, of which Eben was a founding member.

STUART WINTON

A graduate in law from the University of Sheffield, Stuart formerly considered himself a socialist and saw politics as a battle of ideologies, but now feels under siege from politicians of all hues. His pinnacle of personal achievement was to have been a largely inconsequential paper called *The Road to (Taxi) Serfdom – Scotland's £100m Taxi Cartel*, but what should have taken ten weeks is now at ten years and counting.

Okay, we've got the wish list, where's the price list?

Neil Craig
26 November 2013

WITH TODAY'S launch of the Government White Paper the SNP has made these formal promises[1] of what we will get if we vote Yes for separation. These included:

• **Thirty hours of childcare per week in term time for all three and four-year-olds, as well as vulnerable two-year-olds.**

150,000 kids or 200,000 hours so at least another £1 billion in extra taxes. That's 3p on income tax or equivalent the SNP is promising. While childcare in Britain costs[2] over 40.9 per cent of an average wage in Estonia it is only 6.6 per cent. This is because Estonia has a libertarian attitude to freedom. Since Estonia is part of the EU our costs cannot, for once, be blamed on the EU and since Scotland has control over almost all regulation the SNP could reduce these costs to the Estonian level if it really wanted.

• **Trident nuclear weapons, currently based on the Clyde, removed within the first parliament.**

1

Fair enough but what about those working there who will, unless something else is provided, have no jobs.

• **Housing benefit reforms, described by critics as the "bedroom tax", to be abolished, and a halt to the rollout of Universal Credit.**

That is another promise of more spending. My guess another billion.

• **It would be in Scotland's interest to keep the pound, while the Bank of England would continue as "lender of last resort".**

But George Osborne has said he doesn't think it would be in the UK's. It would be possible for Scotland simply to keep using Sterling and let our banks print and attempt to maintain parity without government intervention but this would mean Scotland would not have "gilt edged" government borrowing.

The real problem is that as "lender of last resort" the BoE is guaranteeing Scottish government debt and it is obvious why that is unattractive. Since we would be taking our share of the national debt the Scottish government will have debt to be guaranteed. Certainly there is no way a BoE would ever guarantee a higher borrowing rate in Scotland than in the UK and if our economy was shaky the fiscally proper thing for them to do would be to demand we borrow less – something which all Keynesians will recognise a problem with.

The fact that oil prices swing wildly make it absolutely certain that Scottish government revenue will do so as well, meaning that the ability to borrow to smooth the curves is vital.

• **BBC Scotland replaced at the start of 2017 with a new Scottish broadcasting service, continuing a formal relationship with the rest of the BBC.**

What sort of "independent" country allows a foreign country to control its broadcasting? While it is true that the BBC has a legal duty of "balance" (A) it makes no attempt to keep to it and (B) there are bound to be circumstances where balance means something different to a Scottish audience.

For example if UKIP became a part, or the whole, of the rest of UK government a balanced BBC would be forced to cover their policies and, for example, give significant airtime to reporting that the catastrophic warming fraud is indeed a fraud. Seeing Salmond's enthusiastic support for the fascistic thugs who attacked Nigel Farage and him promising we will be 100 per cent on intermittent "renewables" by 2020 is it conceivable that his Scottish government could put up with an English definition of balance in state owned media?

• Basic rate tax allowances and tax credits to rise at least in line with inflation.

Yet we know that over a fairly long term revenue from oil will decline and the proportion of pensioners rise. That means that, other things being equal, taxes must rise unless there is a reduction in state activity – but the SNP promises to extend it.

• A safe, "triple-locked" pension system.

This is a post dated cheque on what, if the IFS report is right, is a declining bank[3]. At the very least it would mean billions more in taxes.

• Minimum wage to "rise alongside the cost of living".

Take that as you want. The SNP's partners in the Yes campaign have promised there will be no increase in living standards for 10 years, hopefully longer (their hope not mine). Anyway this is another post dated cheque.

This White Paper looks like costing about £2 billion in extra taxes immediately (6p on income tax or some unspecified alternative) with more to come, which along with a far higher electricity prices here because we are 100 per cent renewable (not to mention blackouts for the same reason) seems an improbable launching pad for the growth which is the only way the IFS predictions of us being smothered in higher pensioner costs and lower oil revenue would be prevented.

I do not dispute that Scotland could grow faster than the UK, if it adopted sane free market economic and energy policies and quit the only zone of the world in recession, the EU (or indeed that the UK could grow faster than the UK is doing currently by the same method). But there is no sign of any such sanity in any part of the Holyrood consensus.

[1] *http://www.bbc.com/news/uk-scotland-scotland-politics-25088251*
[2] *http://a-place-to-stand.blogspot.co.uk/2013/03/childcare.htm*
[3]*Ghandi's description of the British WW2 offer of post war independence to India.*

We can be proud to be British (and Glaswegian) too!

Ivor Tiefenbrun
28 November 2013

I DO NOT object to nationalist pride, but I can feel that way and still live in the Union as a proud Scot.

And, anyway, the SNP want us to be ruled by Europe instead of being in a closer and proven joint venture with the other three of the four British Nations. I want to know what the reason is for separation other than the absurd claim that by losing a £1200 per year per head of population advantage we will all be £600 better off. Oh Really! But even if true, so what?

I am a Glasgow (and also proud of that) manufacturer who founded his own company that is world renowned, for performance and technical innovation and market leadership, and we mark all our Made in the United Kingdom products as being "Clyde Built", and furthermore we design and precision engineer them all in Glasgow using our own skilled labour, specialised software, original circuit topographies and innovative designs, rather than outsourcing to China or other so called low-cost locations.

5

We sell less than one per cent of what we make in Scotland, which is fairly typical of most of our World Class Companies, and like most other Scottish manufacturers we export the balance, with England and the rest of the UK being our biggest market. *Why would we want to alienate our biggest customers?*

Who thinks it would be a good idea to have two separate and different, *indeed independent*, tax, PAYE and VAT systems and separate employment law and pension regulations etc., for our Scottish and English, Welsh and Irish, employees? Who thinks we would not lose business and tourist trade if we separated or that any separation would not be acrimonious? Who believes in amicable one sided divorces that have no unpleasant consequences?

Who can give me any tangible economic upside to separation that counteracts these massive disadvantages? The short answer is nobody can, because there is no upside for Scottish businesses, unless perhaps if you seek to be a favoured supplier to the Scottish Government of windmills or old age care or similar – but EU competition laws should preclude any such favouritism. For this reason and to avoid that debate over the economic costs of separation we are repeatedly told, by the Separatists, that we will all be better off, with more jobs and better pensions and more hand outs with lower taxes and better education and health etc., but with no supporting facts to back up this unbelievable and contradictory disinformation.

So, why given the vast array of devolved powers the SNP now controls are we not already living in a real Paradise as opposed to being sold a dream that fools no-one?

What more powers do we need? The right to declare war without the means to defend ourselves? The right to posture and grandstand without cause or responsibilities?

Grow up Scotland, we can be more independent as part of a free Union we did so much to make great and for which we and our British partners can be truly proud.

The White Paper and Trident: just how enterprising are the nationalists, really?

Andrew Morrison
28 November 2013

ONE OF the main assumptions the proponents of independence often make is that Scots are fundamentally opposed to a nuclear deterrent. CND says we are, for the most part; Lord Ashcroft's polling featured in *The New Statesman* says we aren't.

It goes without saying an independent Scotland would not have an independent nuclear deterrent. Even if we wanted one, it would simply be too expensive for a nation with just over five million people to pay for. It doesn't even feature as a discussion point if next year's referendum delivers a Yes result.

Many polls – although there are others to the contrary – show a majority in Scotland opposing a replacement for Trident. That is an entirely different proposition to what the SNP set out in its white paper, which is to remove the presence of nuclear weapons from Scotland's soil entirely.

That is a more extreme view, held by those in independence

movement but not by a majority of the public. As with other issues in this campaign so far, these more radical views have been purposefully misrepresented in a way to try and make them tie in with the wider views of the people. The Nationalists have also tried it with welfare reform, but again many polls show the majority of Scots actually support these.

Even assuming Scots don't want to spend money on nuclear weapons, demanding these weapons are not present in Scotland is a different question. Being able to charge Westminster an extortionate rent to continue basing Trident at Faslane is an entirely different proposition altogether, and one that a truly enterprising government would pursue further.

The fact this option has been absent so far makes one question exactly what balance the SNP has between mature, mainstream and level headed politicians and the far-left, pacifist, anti-NATO, anti-capitalist crazies.

Instead of banishing a modern, safe weapons system from the country's borders with the zeal and candour of a university students' CND branch, a mature and responsible Government would consider what opportunities could arise from the rest of the UK lacking a suitable alternative base.

Considering the rest of the UK has no suitable locations in the pipeline for an alternative, Scotland would hold all the cards. This would be a way for Scotland to retain the jobs dependent on Trident's presence, raise a sizeable amount of revenue for spending on public services or to fund tax cuts, and not pay a single penny piece towards nuclear weapons.

One idea touted in June this year by the Scotland Institute would be that Faslane and the surrounding area would remain UK soil after independence, as part of the negotiations between the Scottish Government and Westminster. Technically, the pacifist crazies would have fulfilled their pledge – no nukes on Scotland's soil, for that part within Scotland would on paper remain British soil – but that is a fudge.

Surely the other proposition is a win-win situation, right? If £500 either way a year makes a material difference to whether Scots would vote for independence or not, then this is a fact the naive element of the Yes campaign (the sizeable part of it) ought to face up to. As a committed Unionist in both head and heart, I am relieved that this is a very unlikely prospect.

After all, what if the worst were to happen? A rogue nuclear attack on the British deterrent – even if that base were in the deepest South of England, Scotland would be similarly crippled by the fallout from such a blast. There were recorded incidents of radiation poisoning from a relatively small meltdown in Chernobyl after all. A radiation cloud would not stop and turn back at Hadrian's Wall.

A very conservative estimated rental of £500m a year for Faslane would generate enough additional revenue to give every basic rate taxpayer a tax cut of £200 per year. And £500m is a very modest estimate considering the predicament the UK Government would be in, and the exorbitant costs the UK MoD would incur relocating the base entirely once a suitable alternative was found.

The SNP would never go for such a pragmatic policy, because it is not a pragmatic party. The SNP activists would never accept such a policy, the SNP backbench would never vote for such a policy. The reasonably moderate MSPs pushing through NATO was hard enough, costing them (choosing my words generously) two MSPs.

Most Scots don't see Trident as a red-line issue of importance the same way the pro-Yes campaigners do. Some hardline Yes campaigners think Trident is a good enough issue to vote for independence alone. They'll never connect with the swing voters the way they need to with that attitude.

Scots are canny, and yes, often say why pay for something you'll never use when you can recruit more nurses, build more schools, etc. which I accept is an argument against replacing

Trident even if I don't agree with it. But those same canny Scots would say if we can use Trident to generate extra money for extra nurses and schools, then go for it, and wouldn't understand saying no to additional revenue on a point of principal. Left wing governments have demonstrated decade after decade that principals don't pay for policies.

The main flaw with the White Paper, in so far as I've been able to read it so far, is that it reads more like a manifesto for an SNP government than a prospectus for independence, thus it is informed by the opinion of an immoderate SNP backbench and activist base. The short-sighted policy on Trident is only one such example of this.

So exactly what assurances can the Scottish people infer from the SNP position on this issue that they would be sensible, pragmatic and canny on any other issue?

The hope in the hype

James Corbett
29 November 2013

WHAT A PIECE of work that was!

Once I started reading, I just couldn't put it down. It has been a long time since anything I've read has provoked such a strong emotional response. Tuesday's publication of this document will live in people's memories for some time to come.

Yes, Joan McAlpine's latest column in the Daily Record has certainly got people talking.

On a day when most of us were preparing ourselves for stratospheric hyperbole levels, Joan set the bar high before the doors of the Glasgow Science Centre were even unlocked. In her column titled *"Who do you trust with Scotland's Future?"*, we were treated to several hundred words of whatever the opposite of expectation management is.

The most memorable comment is that the Scottish Government white paper *"makes America's historic Declaration of Independence look like a Post-it note."*

Wow.

That does of course raise the question of George Washington's status compared to the First Minister (a colonial wee nyaff wi' nae ambition); or how JFK's oration compares to

Nicola Sturgeon's (Details, man! I need a comprehensive list of exactly what I can do for my country?).

Call that a dream Mr King? Sure, your children being judged not by the colour of their skin, but by the content of their character is all very well – but will they grow up in a land free of the "bedroom tax" and Tories? I think not. The Communist Manifesto (20 pages of A4) is of little political or cultural influence compared to *"Scotland's Future"*. The Bible? A mere bagatelle. How small Moses must feel, knowing that he only gave the people Ten Commandments but Alex Salmond brought forth 650 answers. Probably just as well the Scottish Government opted for paper rather than stone tablets.

Oddly, the hype gives me hope. Not for nationalists but for supporters of the UK. A big part of the SNP's electoral success has come from tightly controlling the narrative and their own MSPs. The upper echelons of the pro-independence campaign know that the only way to secure a victory is to present independence to the public as a natural progression rather than a radical change; an evolution rather than a revolution. *"Scotland's Future"* is supposed to be a business proposal rather than a religious proclamation.

Grandiose statements about independence by the more fervent but less prominent nationalists are exactly what those at the top of the campaign want to avoid. There can be no suggestion of serious risks with independence, no worries that the divorce proceedings would be extremely complicated or acrimonious. There must be no impression that post-independence there would be big changes to the more sacred institutions like the Queen or the pound.

The only changes must be what the majority would consider changes for the better; an end to the "bedroom tax", halting the roll out of Universal Credit, providing more free childcare, cutting energy bills and a more generous welfare system. The most acceptable form of independence is one that doesn't introduce too much uncertainty or major change into the lives of voters. Independence must be small "c" conservative.

Winston Churchill said that "the best argument against democracy is a five-minute conversation with the average voter". It may be that the best argument against independence is a five minute conversation with a committed nationalist who isn't working to a script.

Alex Massie observed in his *Spectator* blog that the launch of *"Scotland's Future"* moved the idea of independence closer to the mainstream. The polished, sober presentation given by Salmond and Sturgeon aimed to make independence a credible, even sensible alternative. One of the big risks for Yes Scotland as the referendum date draws nearer is that they can simply no longer contain the wilder strains of nationalism behind the approachable, acceptable surface.

The nationalism of bitterness. The nationalism which accuses its opponents of treachery, insanity or stupidity. The nationalism driven not purely by a love of Scotland, but also a hatred of the UK. The nationalism, that is, that no-one would vote for.

There's a mindset among some of the most vocal advocates of independence that just doesn't gel with the wider electorate. The accusation most frequently levelled by nationalists is that those who wish to remain in the UK believe Scotland is "too wee, too poor, and too stupid" to be independent. In reality there is an increasingly loud strand of nationalism that believes Scotland is just too rich, too enlightened and just too damned important to the future of the world not to be independent.

Who, then, will refuse Scotland anything? Unfortunately in a negotiated settlement, both sides have to give something. At the moment, the nationalists' "gives" are unclear. Evidently the Spanish Government (which isn't a big fan of separatists) has no plans to start hoovering the red carpet in readiness for Scotland's arrival in the EU. Is it so crazy to assume that other countries will have their own concerns and objections?

In The Gettysburg Address (another Post-it worthy document), Abraham Lincoln expressed the hope that *"government of the people, by the people, for the people shall not perish from the earth"*, but can Yes Scotland be quite so confident of their ambitions?

How the SNP's big week went sour

Murdo Fraser
30 November 2013

THIS TUESDAY was the "Yes Campaign" for Scottish independence's big opportunity to make a difference in the seemingly endless referendum campaign. For years we have been told that the SNP Government's White Paper would provide all the answers to people's questions on what independence would mean. The publication date of Tuesday was eagerly awaited.

The burden of expectation was certainly high. All the uncertainty created by those who wish to keep the UK together over issues such as EU membership, currency, the energy market, and a whole host of other matters, have undoubtedly damaged the Yes campaign. This was their, and the SNP's, big chance to change the game.

In advance of Tuesday's announcements, I and many of my unionist colleagues were concerned that the SNP would pull some rabbit out of the hat; that there would be some unexpected announcement of significant new information that might shift public opinion. In the event, our fears proved groundless.

The launch itself seemed to be a rather low key, somewhat flat occasion. Alex Salmond was not his usual ebullient self. Perhaps this was deliberate. Certainly there was nothing in the White Paper to advance the SNP's separatist cause one iota. There were no rabbits, just the same old repeated assertions.

So we are no further forward in terms of detailed information as to whether there will be a currency union post independence, or as to how, and on what terms, an independent Scotland might become a member of the EU. There are certainly plenty of words in the White Paper, some 650 pages' worth, but none that provides substantially new information.

And the document just exposes some of the inherent contradictions in the SNP position. A very good example of this is an issue I have raised on various occasions over the past two years, namely the question of Scotland's financial services industry. The biggest concern that industry has about independence is that there would need to be a separate Scottish financial regulator, and that different regulatory rules in Scotland would create major administrative burdens for companies headquartered here, whose major customer base is south of the Border.

The section in the White Paper on financial services regulation does accept (as it has to under EU law) that there would be a separate Scottish regulator, but tries to give assurances that regulation would be kept closely in line with that elsewhere in the UK. But just turn the page and you find something directly contradictory. There is a passage railing against the actions of payday lenders, and against the UK government for not taking action against them (of course this pre-dated last week's announcement from the Treasury of about capping excessive interest rates), and a pledge to bring in stricter regulation.

So, on the one hand we are being promised regulations that will stay the same, but within a few paragraphs we are being told that in this area at least regulations would be made stricter. And this is precisely the problem with having a separate regulatory regime; over time, with political demands, there would bound to be divergence. No-one in the financial services industry will be the least bit reassured by what was in the White Paper.

Nor was there any greater clarity when it came to the question of energy. The subsidies to fund Scotland's renewable energy industry currently are spread across 60 million electricity consumers across the UK. There is absolutely no certainty as to what would happen to these subsidies in the event of independence. Would consumers down south still be prepared to pay these subsidies to what would then be a foreign country? The only answer to this is that this would be a "reasonable consideration". Anyone thinking of investing in renewable energy in Scotland should take careful note.

Don't expect much detail on Scotland's financial situation in the event of independence. No financial projections are given for any years after 2016/17. In the wake of the recent Institute for Fiscal Studies' report on the financial challenges facing an independent Scotland, it is surprising, to say the least, that this aspect was not specifically addressed.

There was one eye-catching announcement at the launch, and that was the pledge of extended state-funded childcare. The obvious retort from unionist parties was: as this is a devolved matter, why don't you just go on and do this now? The convoluted response from the SNP about where the tax benefits from increased female participation in the workforce would then go, simply didn't convince.

It also left the question unanswered as to what would happen if Scotland voted "Yes" to independence, but the SNP then lost the subsequent election. Anyone voting for independence simply to get better childcare would therefore be disappointed. The fact is that no rational person could or should vote for irreversible constitutional change simply on the basis that it might lead to the introduction of one particular policy, which itself might easily be reversed within a matter of years.

The SNP needed a game-changer in the independence debate, and this certainly wasn't it. With the Spanish Prime Minister's hugely significant intervention on Wednesday evening suggesting that an independent Scotland might not find entry into the EU a smooth process, what should have been a triumphant week for the Yes campaign turned very sour.

I seriously doubt that the 650-odd pages of the White Paper will have won independence a single extra vote. Seldom have so many trees died in vain.

White Paper: leaden prose, intellectually thin and shoddy construction

Hugh Andrew
2 December 2013

IF THE First Minister had popped in to ask me to publish a book setting out the case for an independent Scotland and my company's advice as to how to do it then I would have given him the following thoughts. After all communication is our business.

Firstly I would start with a 'vision' piece. It should be both personal and beautifully crafted. It should make a limited number of key points and endeavour to come up with simple memorable phrases for each of them. Those phrases would form the basis of the campaign.

There should then be a 'tour d'horizon' of where Scotland is. Crucially that section should build a historical picture as well. We should be able to see long trends in our country and where they lead. So tables and graphs would be necessary but can of course be put in appendices or footnotes where too much technicality is involved. This section should endeavour to highlight 'difference' and 'divergence' between Scotland and England. It should thus illustrate without needing to state how 'one size fits all' policy increasingly works less and less. One could also (without labouring the point) give a feeling of historical inevitability to the whole process from the formation of the Scottish Office to the current day Scotland has been steadily moving along one path and thus one more step is all that is needed.

The third section should look at the powers the Scottish Parliament currently has and the extra powers that 'independence' would give it as well as what those powers would mean in terms of increased room for activity.

And the fourth could then look at what a 'Scottish' approach might be. If the FM had suggested putting in lots of detailed policies I would strongly have advised him against. This is a paper above party and should not contain party proposals – and secondly, so to do says much about two things – one the inappropriate conflation of party and government , a hostage to fortune for your enemies; and also the areas where you clearly have no detailed policy proposals.

Far better too in a document that should be as broad and inclusive in its tone as possible to indicate directions of travel rather than destinations with all the problems of detail and argument that those can incur.

But there needs to be a fifth and a clear section. The Scottish government should be fully open and honest about the difficulties and the grey areas in negotiations. It should be clear that there is much that cannot be known or assumed and some of these represent major matters – currency and Europe being two. It should be clear too that these CANNOT be known in advance. Neither Europe nor the UK government, quite rightly, will lay their hands out. Being open about this again shows that this is not an SNP paper but a paper of the government of Scotland. Attempting to hide problematic issues through assertion or dogmatic statement is something that a cynical electorate will see right through.

And then in an Epilogue I would look at the whole changing history of the UK and present this as part of that evolution. Powers have gone and are continuing to go to Wales and Northern Ireland for instance, Scotland is merely further down the road. I would soothe and comfort an electorate for whom this might seem a revolutionary proposal. I would point up the huge links that Scotland has with the rest of the UK and how independence represents an adjustment but not an attempt to fracture these.

Finally I would tell him that the whole thing needs accomplished in around 80,000 words – or 288pp max. It has got to be readable.

You might gather from the above that the First Minister did not seek my advice.

What we have is an overlong deeply repetitive piece of turgid prose awash with non sequiturs which veers alarmingly from macro aspiration to micro detail. Awkward issues are repeatedly glossed over. Much of it is de facto an SNP manifesto indicating an alarming level of collusion with the civil service. As a 'call to votes' it is singularly lacking. So what does the content say?

Firstly it suggests that the SNP has little deeply rooted sense of why it wants independence. One of the most striking things about it is the repeated statements as to how well Scotland is performing in the Union. Indeed outside London we appear to be by far the best performing part of it.

Having got independence, policy seems to be merely touching the tiller in a deeply conservative direction. All the Coalition changes within social security will be reversed if they represent constraint and kept if they represent growth. With regard to tax there is a tip of the hat to Sir John Mirrlees but only in the sense of vague talk of simplification. Interesting indeed is that all the Mirrlees reports' most radical proposals appear to have been shorn out. Business tax might be cut but that is merely aspirational and how interesting that the wild talk of slashing corporation tax has been replaced with a more judicious 3 per cent reduction.

With regard to thorough reforms of the constitution internally well there is really very little. Local government and local democracy rate little mention. Issues such as the concentrations of power in Scottish society never raise their ugly head. Indeed rather like Dr Pangloss one might think that it really requires very little to make this 'the best of all possible worlds'. Whole sections appear to be just codged in from other reports or documents. So 'culture' is essentially Blair Jenkins' broadcasting report and a few vague notions tacked on. A cynic might remark that apart from a general belief that culture is a 'good thing' the SNP appears to have no policy.

So the absences in the report and the obvious seams in its construction say much more than perhaps the SNP would find comfortable about the party and its thinking. What it does have, however, is very clear ideas on is spending. Indeed we have a flood of precise spending commitments, even if vaguely costed. The party clearly is still much more comfortable with the concept of distributing pork than working out how to breed pig.

It is unlikely, however, that vast bulk of the Scottish population will grit their teeth and read it. Perhaps that indeed is the aspiration, to create a codex so dense and so badly laid out that one can wave it and say 'the answer is here' in the sure knowledge no one will find it even if it is. I wonder if that is too cynical an interpretation and perhaps an even more worrying one presents itself. That this document – in its intellectual thinness, in its shoddy construction, in its leaden prose represents the true face of Scottish government – the endless production of policies which rather like the *Sorcerers Apprentice* replicate themselves and march endlessly up and down the steps without point or purpose but give a seeming air of activity on a much deeper stagnation.

In this 'White paper' the SNP is merely demonstrating it is the latest in a long line of parties in Scotland where the act of governing seems to produce an almost terminal intellectual sclerosis about the purpose of governance. It is not the aspiration of independence which chills me to the marrow, it is the depressing and enervating conservatism contained within that aspiration.

Hugh Andrew is managing director of Birlinn Publishing, Scotland's largest independent publisher.

Fifty shades of grey – all pain but nothing sexy

Vivian Linacre
2 December 2013

IS THIS a White Paper – or is it Fifty Shades of Grey? Why is the response to almost every simple question, even after two years of campaigning – and, supposedly, research – not the expected definite answer but a vague "should not be affected" or "unlikely to change" or "may not allow"; and why, conversely, is the response to almost every complex question, to which nobody can possibly yet know the answer, presented as if it were an accomplished fact: e.g. agreements for EU and for NATO membership, for a sterling union, sharing the National Debt and maritime resources?

So it is a hybrid monster: neither – as had been promised – an objective set of proposals prepared by civil servants nor a political party manifesto, but the latter dressed up as the former.

An historically important publication by HMG, but with no references to sources, no citations. Wholesale assertions are made without the slightest attempt at authoritative backing. Is this mere incompetence or have they wilfully failed to do their homework

25

Why, in particular, has no draft constitution been prepared? It is a case of 'Never mind the quality: feel the width!'

But we may yet be in for a series of what the tabloids are sure to call 'Jock Shocks' – the first of which is that, contrary to all the polls and pundits, the SNP may actually win the referendum!

For four reasons: more voting Yes will bother to turn out than those voting No, particularly among the juveniles; the chauvinistic boost provided by the Glasgow Commonwealth Games, Ryder Cup and Battle of Bannockburn 700th anniversary; visceral hatred of Tories and dreadful leadership by all three opposition parties; but above all because of a probable decline in the economy between now and next September, arousing popular protest and unrest which can only find expression in vilifying Westminster and suppressing support for the status quo.

As the UK government in 2012 spent £120bn more than it collected in taxes and public debt is heading towards the trillion mark – half as much again since the coalition came to power barely three years ago – with no sign of diminishing, what if the international credit agencies downgrade the pound again, compelling the Governor of the Bank of England to raise base rate to 1.50 per cent, or even 2.00 per cent, wiping billions of capital off banks' balance sheets and causing an inflationary surge which would harm every household and a rise in mortgage interest rates that could precipitate another crash in the housing market?

After a quarter century of falling interest rates, which has coincided with – and been exploited by – a quarter century of public profligacy, might this long-term trend be overdue for reversal, and would not that cause general alarm or even panic – and a million Scots to feel like getting out?

But even if a provisional government is formed, it will all end in tears.

Eight months after the Referendum a UK General Election will be held which, if the economy continues to suffer, could be won by Labour, who will feel no obligation to collaborate with the nationalist Scottish government in resolving the many issues still in dispute. The SNP and Labour will fight with special ferocity, moreover, because 59 constituencies, 40 of them held by Labour, would disappear at Independence Day, 24th March 2016, upon inauguration of the new State.

That Westminster campaign and its aftermath will make inroads on the eighteen months allowed for the entire process from a successful referendum to Independence Day – a period which the SNP leaders had always declared ample for conduct and conclusion of negotiations with the EU and NATO, Treasury, Home and Foreign Offices, and for setting up the many other essential institutions of government; but in reality would prove hopelessly inadequate.

Moreover, apportionment of the exploding National Debt, bifurcation of the NHS and of state pension liabilities and administration, and the future of the House of Lords, among many other salient issues, would absorb vast resources while remaining intractable. By the winter of 2015-16 the political climate could become extremely embittered, too, by the first wave of power cuts owing to a predicted energy crisis which will be largely blamed on Scotland's proclaimed but failing reliance on 'renewables', further discrediting the party that, although in power, was seen to be incapable of generating it!

Consequently, they would overrun the appointed date for nationhood and Holyrood would be compelled to plead with Westminster for deferment of Independence Day until *after* the Scottish parliamentary elections that are due in May '16 – only two months away – and cannot be postponed! Obviously, a total span of twenty months between referendum and general elections was always absurdly short.

A White Paper, full of meat but free of fat, could have been brought out a year ago and all the issues fully explored before next September. The plan to bring out the White Paper, then do nothing but argue about it for a whole year until the referendum and then go like crazy to get through more than two years' work in eighteen months through UK elections never made sense.

The Scottish government's humiliation – the ultimate 'Jock Shock' – would be revelled in by the opposition parties. The administration would try to put a good face on it by seeking a fresh mandate from the people to defeat 'the enemies of sovereignty' in order to come back and 'finish the job'. But having apparently deserted Scotland's 'Date with Destiny' when the long-planned opportunity presented itself – having failed this crucial test of competency – its downfall would be inevitable and the grand illusion of independence shattered. So what was it all about?

September '14, May '15, March '16 and May '16 – a deadly serious game of 'Hopscotch'!

An Oil Fund would not have been possible in the 70s and 80s

Brian Monteith
2 December 2013

There are moments when I recall my youth as a conservative student in the dying days of Jim Callaghan's government and the dawn of what was called Thatcherism as if it was only last week, and yet so much of then appears to have been rather conveniently forgotten as our recent history is reshaped to fit the narrative of today's politicians.

I am reminded of the day in 1980 I first attended a national meeting of the Scottish Young Conservatives and found to my horror that the new prime minister's chief opposition would come not from Labour politicians and trade unionists – but from a fifth column in the party's own ranks that at every opportunity was keen to cut a deal with collectivists and sue for peace.

It was not that such feint-hearts were especially marshalled to defeat her (although they did have a sort of old-boys-in tweed-skirts network) it was simply that the prevailing mindset of the Scottish Conservative establishment was disposed towards the received wisdom of state intervention. This included public ownership of industry being in the national interest, applying a prices and incomes policy to fight Labour's cost of living crisis and almost daily state involvement in solving industrial disputes.

A motion called on Margaret Thatcher to put yet more taxpayers money into failing Clydeside shipyards, and although it was defeated after a close debate, it was a precursor to similar appeals from many Scottish Conservatives for her to intervene and save other nationalised enterprises; save Gartcosh, save Ravenscraig, save the coal mines and take other such initiatives that would show the Conservatives cared about Scotland.

My point here is not to defend Thatcher's actions – that is for another time – but to illustrate that if the Conservative Prime Minister was under such incessant pressure from within her own ranks then one can more easily appreciate the default position of the Scottish political establishment, most newspaper editorials and media commentary. State intervention in the economy had been accepted and repeatedly justified by all parties since the end of the last war and whenever a new problem surfaced it was the first response of most politicians.

It is important to understand just how suffocating, how perfidious this view was in the 70s and 80s to understand why there never was such a thing as an Oil Fund, established for the benefit of the UK, or solely Scotland, in the future.

That the tax revenues accruing from oil exploration and production from chiefly Scottish waters went to the UK Treasury is not disputed, nor is the fact that they were used in part to underwrite an economic transformation to a more modern British economy that might pay its way. What is forgotten is just how often those revenues were used to help adjust the change that was required in Scotland, all the more so because it had a greater concentration of heavy industries that were being priced out of existence from global competition.

Some argue that was a squandering of public wealth, that had Scotland been independent we could have garnered our own Oil

Fund to match that of Norway's. Such an attitude ignores the nature of Scotland's past economy and is to presuppose that all those state-owned and generally loss-making steelyards, shipyards, mines and railway engineering shops would have somehow ceased to be a drain on the public purse if Thatcherism stopped at Hadrian's Wall.

Oil revenues could most certainly have gone into a fund that might grow and the interest be used for the benefit of future Scottish economic demands, but the state investment in closures, including retraining, environmental clean-up, locate in Scotland hand-outs, new business start-ups and general improvement in infrastructure – not to mention the welfare benefits to ease the pain – could not have been afforded at the same time.

Indeed, had so many of the factory names that are now little more than proud memories or our industrial folklore been encouraged to continue, the very politicians that now tell us we should have had an Oil Fund are the very same people that back then would have been at the front of the queue demanding state money be used for the good of this or that threatened Scottish industry.

We would be told it had a strategic importance, that Scotland would somehow be incomplete without such an industry, that our nation could yet be a world leader again, that thousand of jobs needed saving as well as thousands more that supplied them.

It would not end with the ailing state industries, for such a mindset sees little distinction between public and private such as Bathgate (public) and Linwood (private) and does not baulk at throwing taxpayers' money at enterprises others believe a bad investment.

If you doubt this you just have to go back to the news reporting of those times and you will find demands being made upon the Conservative government to step in and save such enterprises. This was not an entirely Scottish pursuit, similar demands were made for industrial rescue in Merseyside,

Wearside, Wales and the Midlands – but the idea that having both state intervention and a growing Oil Fund would have been possible is a fiction peculiar to Scotland.

All of this is important for as Alex Salmond, Nicola Sturgeon and John Swinney take us down our own road road to Damascus we are being told that Scotland can now have an Oil Fund that will be of great benefit to future generations. And yet these are the same people that have shown a startling willingness to step forward to save Prestwick airport and were prepared to consider all options to save Grangemouth's Ineos petrochemical plant in a world of surplus capacity.

We are being offered political promises by people that have a record of not keeping them, or when they do, of bad management and catalogued failures. Independence should be more than that, it should be about liberty from subjugation, self determination and constitutional protection from over-governance – precisely the opposite route that the SNP is offering to take us in its White Paper.

It is one thing to suggest an independent Scotland would have an Oil Fund, it is to deny past experience for the same politicians to pretend they would not seek to raid it at the slightest hint of economic trouble.

Being Scottish in Team GB benefits us all

Liz Smith
2 December 2013

WITH ALL the hullabaloo of last week's White Paper, it would be very easy to overlook some of the statements contained in the lengthy Q&A section at the back of the document. For example, the answer to question 223 might not be seen in the same context as the answers which are supposed to resolve what will happen to our tax, our pensions and our currency, but it sure matters to our elite athletes and aspiring Olympians and therefore to the very sizeable proportion of the Scottish public interested in sport.

On the surface, answer 223 tells us what we have known for some time; that Alex Salmond wants to have a Team Scotland at the Olympics, but, read more closely, and we find an extraordinary admission; "Whilst the Scottish Government hopes that all athletes who are qualified to represent Scotland will do so, this is a personal decision." In other words, there would be a Team Scotland and a Team GB and athletes would be free to choose which one they would like to compete in, providing, of course, they met the relevant qualifying criteria.

This is just plain daft. Where on earth is the logic of some athletes choosing to compete in the Olympics for Team Scotland

and some choosing to compete for Team GB? Both teams would surely lose out and therefore seriously weaken their overall medal chances on the world stage. It does not make sense.

But then, maybe it doesn't matter too much since it sounds as though most of our athletes have already made up their minds. Almost to a man and a woman they would choose team GB. For the most part, this would be nothing whatsoever to do with their political opinions, and everything to do with sport and achieving the best results for their country and their fellow team members.

Listen to Andy Murray or Chris Hoy or Katherine Grainger or any of the other recent Olympic medallists, and there is a common theme. They will tell you that one of the reasons they have been able to get where they are in sport is because of their regular access, often over many years, to first class UK facilities. Sometimes these might be based in Scotland – and we will no doubt see more of them after Glasgow 2014 – but more often than not, they are in other parts of the UK - in Manchester, London, Cardiff, Loughborough or wherever.

Whilst training at these venues, elite athletes from Scotland have the facility to work alongside elite athletes from the rest of the UK, not just those from Scotland, and therefore they have a much better opportunity to access these other athletes' support teams and the financial investment which follows them.

Often, that support is substantial and it provides the given sport with the financial economies of scale which it needs to develop both the training facilities and the administration network which are needed for the future. Above all however, it provides them with a long established reputation and the potential to attract world class coaches.

The more extensive the level of competition is, the greater the sporting challenge and the greater the chance of international success. This is not political bias on the part of the athletes or their coaches. It is a statement of fact and it is generally accepted across the UK. Indeed, most of our athletes will tell you that being part of Team GB enhances rather than diminishes their chances of succeeding in Scotland and that it also enhances their pride in being Scottish or English or Welsh or Irish at the same time as being British. If they get asked to wear a Scottish shirt at the Commonwealth Games and a British shirt at the Olympics that is exactly as it should be. They see no contradiction in this – quite the reverse, and they can enjoy both.

Sir Alex Ferguson puts it another way; "I played for Scotland and managed the Scotland team and no-one should question my Scottishness. But 800,000 Scots, like me, live and work in other parts of the UK. We don't live in a foreign country, we are just another part of the family of the UK."

He is very clear indeed, that Scots make the UK stronger and the UK makes Scots feel stronger. Our athletes feel exactly the same and that it is why the answer to question 223 in the White Paper is so absurd.

When Alex Salmond delved into his wife's handbag and unfurled his saltire in the Royal Box at Wimbledon, not only did he look very silly but he also seriously misjudged the public mood. There is nothing in the White Paper which suggests he has learnt the lesson about why.

White Paper: was that it?

Ian Smart
3 December 2013

OVER the previous weekend, in the run up to publication, the length of the White Paper was trailed heavily in the press.

It was to be the most substantial proposal for an independent country ever produced running to 670 pages and covering every possible angle. No one would ever more complain that they did not have enough information.

So I have now read the actual document with something approaching incredulity. 670 Pages with virtually nothing to say.

It is not so much the entirely un-costed wish list of policy promises which even if affordable had no place in what was a Government rather than a Party publication. It is the complete lack of detail on anything of any real importance.

For example, as a lawyer, one of the things I was interested in was how the transitional process to independence was anticipated to happen.

We have plenty of experience of such matters in Scotland in recent times. When local government was re-organised in 1974-75 and again in 1994-95, shadow authorities were set up for a year and then power transferred to them after that period. A similar mechanism was adopted when the current Scottish Government created the National Police and Fire Boards.

Now the importance of such transitional arrangements is this. New institutions need management structures, accommodation and above all, staff. And there needs to be the means of recruiting and remunerating these staff until they take on their responsibilities.

An Independent Scotland would need to create such structures on a much larger scale. We'd need an armed forces, a foreign service, and a revenue and customs for a start. And that's just for a start. We'd need to recruit the leaders of such institutions; we'd need them then to create the structures in which they would operate and we'd then need to hire the personnel or at least work out which they would inherit from the UK. Even where that simply (sic) involves the redeployment of existing civil servants there would still be a massive programme of retraining to be undertaken.

And all of that would cost money. Not the sort of mega money that might or might not be there for a fully functioning Scottish state, just the sort of money that would ensure that whoever is answering the phone in the putative Scottish Foreign Office in February 2016 had some way of getting paid at the end of the month.

Now, this could be done, legally, in one of two different ways. The White Paper would concede that technical sovereignty remained with Westminster until "Independence Day" and contain a proposal that Westminster legislate immediately to give the existing Scottish Government the vires to undertake all this hiring etc. Or it could assert that sovereignty would vest in the Scottish Government on the declaration of the referendum result, giving them, if the rest of the world was prepared to play ball, power to act on their own authority in such matters. And it could be paid for in one of two ways. Either by asking Westminster to lend us the money to be repaid after independence (most likely with the first legal route) or, assuming the markets were willing, by borrowing commercially on a promise to repay from sovereign Scottish revenues in due course. (More likely with the second).

So what does the White Paper say? The Executive summary seems to suggest that the first route is the preferred legal one although the document itself is clear as mud. And on financing? Nothing at all. It does indeed have 670 pages but the transition, after 300 years of integration at every level, from the United Kingdom to a sovereign Scotland gets precisely fourteen of them (337-351), even then full of references to transitional "agreements", "negotiations" and "shared services" without a word about what the Scottish Government's objectives would be in these negotiations, let alone whether it has any anticipation of the position of the other side. Let alone (at all) how to pay for this. The cynic might think that last failure applies to much of the rest of the document but at least with that it tried.

But that's not the only example of fundamental but difficult issues being ignored. Take public sector pensions. You have to jump about a bit to find it saying nothing about the difficult bits here.

First of all we have page 149

"In an independent Scotland, all public service pension rights and entitlements which have been accrued for fully or executively devolved or reserved schemes will be fully protected and accessible."

That seems the very least you would expect. But what about those in the Forces and in the non devolved functions of the UK Government currently discharged by Scots, often in Scotland, such as those at DfID in East Kilbride?

Well then we have page 433

"For pension schemes that are currently reserved, such as civil service, armed forces and judicial pensions, the Scottish Government will work with Westminster to ensure an orderly transition of pension responsibilities to an independent Scotland."

What does that mean?

For example:

If I retire from DFiD in February 2016 who pays my pension?

If I did serve in the British forces but am already retired, who pays my pension?

If I worked for the Foreign Office but return to work for the Scottish Foreign Service in 2016 and retire a year later, who pays my pension?

If I've worked for the Scottish Office all my life but am now retired and living in England, who pays my pension?

If I worked for the (wholly English even before Devolution) Department of Education but am now retired and living in Scotland, who pays my pension?

None of the questions are answered or even addressed. Oh but here they are! On page 341

[After a Yes Vote]

"Discussion will also cover the allocation of liabilities, including apportionment of the national debt, the current and future liabilities on public sector pensions, civil nuclear decommissioning and social security benefits."

So that's all right then.

I could choose any number of other examples. The whole document is premised on hypothetical future negotiations in which (as I've observed before) "The English", having treated us appallingly while we are in the same Country, will prove the soul of reasonableness now we want to be in a different country. But worse than that, it assumes that the separation of a unified state of more than 300 years standing would be simpler than even the re-organisation of a Police and Fire Service! In Eighteen months, not only is the whole infrastructure of a State to be created but any number of subsidiary functions such as a Financial Services Regulator. And where that is accepted to be impossible, the assumption is that the rest of the UK will be happy for us to continue to use theirs. 'Cos we love them really.

The truth of this lies in the proposal for Broadcasting. In the sort of dissonant note that you get from a document written by committee, it is accepted that it would be impractical to establish a State Broadcaster any sooner than January 2017. Bizarrely however, that notwithstanding, establishing an entirely new state continues to be maintained as an altogether simpler exercise!

You really do wonder if the SNP leadership regard this whole thing as an entirely serious project?

Indeed, maybe the truth is that they don't. They're not worried about the incoherence of the White Paper as they're already resigned to the conclusion that it has no chance of ever being put to the practical test.

This article was first published on Ian's blog at http://ianssmart.blogspot.co.uk/

Talking dangerous and frightening collectivism to themselves?

Eben Wilson
4 December 2013

LESLEY RIDDOCH, doyenne of the concerned left, complained in *The Scotsman* this week that no-one seemed to want to debate the childcare proposals in the White Paper. She thought it might excite the commentariat more, and be a topic of much scrutiny.

In explanation, she suggested that it might be a "mumsy" subject for a macho media, or that some supporters may be organisationally bound to be impartial and unable to comment, but I think having read the White Paper from start to finish that there are wider reasons. On *ThinkScotland* this week others have pointed to the conservatism and sogginess of what has been offered, I want to look further at the political economy of the choices being offered based on examples from the Health, Wellbeing and Social Protection section that Ms Riddoch will no doubt be most concerned about.

My first example is a fabulous example of what is known as civil service "pudder" from the SNP communications department.

"If in government after the 2016 election, we will adopt a government-wide approach to the health and wellbeing of our nation with confidence that the actions we take, and their success, will be down to our own efforts and our decisions."

Stare at this for a while and your head will hurt. What this means I have no real idea but it seems to mean that when we are independent we will be, er – independent.

What it implies is more important – it's saying that we will have an integrated central plan through which the state will do lots for you. The childcare proposal within this is part of something called "an early years strategy". That's a planned sub-plan within the Big plan.

"we will continue to provide high-quality, world-leading health and social care", "deliver, safe, effective and person-centred services", "continue with current arrangements for the management of the NHS", "look forward to a more personalised package of support", "look forward to our own system of administration for welfare and pensions".

Well, that's fabulous. But what it reflects are a) management-centric choices; "provide", "deliver" "package" and b) self-protective administration: "effective", "arrangements", "personalised", "system".

What this tells us is that the civil service has captured our leaders. Their heads have gone so far into the sinkhole of their bureaucrats plans that they have forgotten what they are there for – to offer confident direction through uncertainties and the management of risks. Offering more childcare is a very comfortable political choice in this managerialist environment.

"not allow changes to the welfare system to be driven by short-term cuts to budgets, but by what is best in the long-term interests of the people of Scotland".

Oh dear, not only captured in mind, but through their wallet too, by "interests". But are these "interests of the people" really chosen by reference to the general interest of the taxpayers? No, political science tells us that they will be choices made by special interests, the very people who manage the plan and develop the strategy.

"Scotland has a greater incidence of cancer and of premature deaths from all causes including heart disease, chronic liver disease and cirrhosis", "1.2 years", "10.9 years", "life expectancy is only 50", "50,000 children will be living in poverty".

Others have noted the weird rapid swerving in the White Paper from the gallant waving of a distemper brush to the concentrated minutiae of a camel-hair. What I see is meaningless quack science, a classic ruse of choice by the bureaucracy desperate to justify its plans. Some of these diseases are genetic, their aetiology and epidemiology are seriously complicated. Some are self-imposed. How does this guide policy choices – it can't – other than a few well-researched clinicians the state may have discretion but it is sadly ignorant. We've been trying to resolve these issues for many years. The political choice here is a common one; the plan to reduce health and other inequalities has failed, and we just need more planning and resources to mend that failure.

"An independent Scotland will not replicate the economic structure of the UK; instead independence will bring opportunities to operate more effectively and efficiently", "goal of equality and fairness".

Yet more puff and guff of course – what exactly is the economic structure of the UK? I think this might be leftist shorthand for "we don't like capitalism". And of course we want government to do what it says it will do, and do it well. But what is hidden between the lines here is the assumption that "equality" and "fairness" are *de facto* definable and also desirable.

This is where I begin to get worried; Utopian promises of free child care and other free lunches come from this attitude. By definition, more is good, less is bad – with no unintended consequences. This ignores the observable reality from the Soviet period that an entire society can be poor in a richly-resourced country where government equalises everyone because they choose to judge fairness politically. In a democracy they can achieve this through high and over-progressive taxation. It's more than likely that will be needed to pay for the childcare dream.

"The social investment model fosters a culture in society that is more inclusive, more respectful and more equal. It also places the cash transfers that people traditionally think of as welfare – such as out of work benefits and tax credits – in a wider, more cost-effective and socially beneficial context when viewed over the longer-term."

I think this is one of the most frightening sentences I have read for a long time. We have to presume that it is the state that is in charge in this investment model. So it is the state that fosters, seeks respectfulness and equality, and engineers a socially beneficial context.

This investment then is red in tooth and claw mandatory socialism.

The cultural hegemony of collective endeavour that has destroyed free spirit wherever it has been tried. And no doubt they will want to apply it to our children first, through state sponsored, registered and regulated childcare centres. Truly dangerous.

So, Ms Riddoch, why has their not been much debate about the childcare proposal?

1) It's a sub-section of a central plan that ignores the fact that central planning does not work and cannot work. See Von Mises.

2) It's a managerial measure based on self-serving expediency, it assumes perpetual disadvantage and offers no direction out of that. See Murray Rothbard.

3) Its monolithic nature will induce capture by special interests and bureaucratic sclerosis. See James Buchanan.

4) It's based on false scientism that offers data as statistical fact that is not fact, just data of unknown quality or importance and unhelpful for policy choices. See Friedrich Hayek.

5) It's founded on a view of equality and fairness that is undefined and undefinable, but leaves room for power to corrupt even good people. See Lord Acton.

6) It has the potential for spiritual and economic disaster for a free Scots people. We become wards of a state that thinks it always knows better than us. See George Orwell.

For those who have read the ideas of the scholars above, the idea that we might use the world view of the White Paper and embed it through "social rights" into a written constitution is truly bizarre and genuinely dangerous to our prosperity and freedom.

Why should we engage when these ideas are not taken into account in any way within the White Paper, and when we are totally baffled by this lack of intellectual foundation?

The Declaration of Arbroath tells us that we are free to choose our rulers. I decline to choose those who wrote this until they allow us our freedom.

Scotland in Europe – there is no case without corroboration

Jonathan Stanley
6 December 2013

DISCUSSING the European Union with Nationalists is for many a game of smoke and mirrors. Scotland in Europe has been a cornerstone of the independence debate for over two decades but since the publication of the current SNP manifesto, Scotland's Future, this position's rough edges are being felt on as the 2014 referendum approaches.

We have heard assertions that Scotland will enter a currency union with the rest of the UK, that we are really a Nordic nation in denial, that we will keep our borders open and take our own decisions.

The three parties in Better Together represent a Westminster elite that remains staunchly pro-EU and dare not risk revealing the true extent of the sovereignty Scotland would lose without admitting how much the UK has already lost.

Sir Walter Scott's collection of poems titled Translations and Imitations of German Ballads is a fitting description of how Scotland's laws are made today. Three centuries after the Act of

Union pledged to protect Scots law, 75 per cent of our laws are made by a Brussels bureaucracy in a German dominated Europe. These are transposed into law in Westminster and Holyrood and should we fail to follow these laws we are taken to the European Court of Justice, rather like a trip to the headmaster's office.

This will not be lost on anyone familiar with Rabbie Burns words, "Amoung ourselves united, only by British hands shall Britain's wrangs be righted" because the European Union is the modern day Haughty Gaul. It is a nonsense that a Yes vote would give Scots power to govern ourselves inside the European Union.

The Nationalists should be offering a smorgasbord of currency options based on our Nordic neighbours so they can be considered carefully. That this hasn't been done shows a serious lack of insight into our future currency and little sincerity in building a credible case.

Alex Salmond must be the last man in Europe to believe a political currency union without popular consent for fiscal transfers will do anything but impoverish its peripheral members. England would dominate any BoE decision making and any arguments that the pound is set to suit England would be far more justified than they are today.

Shall we take the Finland option and join the Euro as Scotland would be obliged by the Lisbon Treaty? Perhaps we should take the Swedish option and establish a new central bank and launching our own currency before reapplying. We could go further and have our new currency track the Euro within a very tight band like Denmark does, though her economic cycle is more in line to Eurozone than the UK's. The UK tried keeping within a tight band while tracking the Mark and that brought us economic turmoil called Black Wednesday.

Any of these options inside the EU would commit Scotland to reducing its debt to GDP ratio sustainably as part of the Copenhagen Criteria, the EU's own tests for entry. Given the disaster of letting Greece into the Euro the EU would be extremely strict in applying these conditions today. No new member has ever joined with a national debt as high as Scotland's would be.

We could of course have a new currency and never join the EU, like Norway or Iceland. As we have both oil reserves and a crippled indebted banking sector, Scotland lies economically as well as geographically between these two nations. It seems we are spoiled for choice before even considering the Manx option of having a currency board but this option would mean we would have no monetary control whatsoever, any balancing of the money supply or controlling inflation would have to be done by very brutal fiscal discipline.

John Swinney will need to read the letters of Malachi Malagrowther very carefully before joining the single currency which means signing up to the Eurozone Stability Mechanism, and agreeing to a financial transaction tax that would send Edinburgh's financial sector south of the border. The ESM means Scotland would be liable for billions in Eurozone banking debts, after UK taxpayers alone bailed out our British banks.

Beyond currency and legal jurisdiction a nation needs to control its borders to be independent. To be accountable to its own people it must protect its people's right of association as well as ensuring the local population does not suffer from uncontrolled immigration. When the rest of the UK leaves the EU, Scotland would be the largest English speaking labour market in the EU with a total open door immigration policy, just like Ireland has now.

Given the EU's most taught second language is English there is a dual asymmetry to the freedom of movement that would apply to Scotland in Europe. We are simply richer and have a lower barrier to entry for unskilled workers as the only "Nordic" nation in the EU to speak a global language. With lower wages, higher youth unemployment and no economic sovereignty we are poised to join an Arc of Austerity along with the Eurozone PIIGS rather than master our own future.

Schengen is an obligation of joining the EU and has been since the late 1990s.

The UK opt-out will not apply to Scotland as a new member state yet our current Common Travel Area is a shared asset, an agreement between the UK and Republic of Ireland. Given that Scotland would need the UK and Ireland's approval for joining the EU, a simple opt out, even if negotiated would not be enough. There would have to be a specific exemption from Schengen, for the duration of the CTA, for Scotland to enter the EU. No exemption, rather than opt-out, has ever been granted to an accession country. To iron out these differences by March 2016 is not ambitious: it is risible.

Finally a crucial point was raised at Glasgow University's Turkey in the EU debate recently. How can the EU support the division of Britain that risks letting one nation leave the EU while making it policy to promote the unification of Cyprus? Only a committed pro-EU Nationalist can argue with a straight face for a united Cyprus and divided Britain inside the EU.

Given that our own union is on trial and assertions on the EU have been made by the SNP it is time to call for corroborating evidence. Fortunately, after wasting thousands of pounds hiding its absence, the Scottish Government has commissioned legal advice on Scotland's future relationship with Europe. Without this corroboration, an aspect of Scots law UKIP demands protected, there is no case for Scotland in Europe. Until the Scottish Government releases the legal advice, their policies on Europe are not worth the paper they are printed on.

Senior Tories who say move over Darling could not be more wrong

James Corbett

6 December 2013

THERE ARE many things I could say about Alistair Darling, but I do not think that he was "in a state of deep unconsciousness for a prolonged or indefinite period" would be among them. In a recent article for the *Financial Times*, unnamed senior Tories are reported as saying that Darling is "comatose" and should be replaced at the top of Better Together. I have no doubt that their concerns will be taken very seriously. After all, anyone who thinks the best way to improve a campaign they support is to criticise it in the press, is clearly someone with a deep understanding of politics.

What are we to make of these suggestions that Mr Darling perhaps lacks some of the showmanship and panache of some in the Yes campaign?

I say *good.*

In the face of nationalist hyperactive self righteousness, a cool head is a useful thing to have.

With the launch of the White Paper, the referendum debate has passed an important milestone. There's a feeling among some that "Scotland's Future" will be a game changer for Yes Scotland. It gives it something that its supporters can use as evidence to support their case. It's pretty circumstantial (uncorroborated?) evidence but it's big and tangible and accessible. I've yet to be convinced that the White Paper will somehow transform the debate, but clearly it's entering a new phase.

Independence activists who, let's face it, were a fairly excitable bunch to begin with have been whipped into something of a frenzy since the launch. For senior nationalists in the media spotlight, they no longer have to rely on hugely complicated reports or merely stating that they believe their position is an entirely acceptable one, they have something official, written in black and white to back them up. Expect many of the answers to probing questions about independence to be prefaced with "If you look at page ... of the White Paper..."

Considering Alistair Carmichael's recent mauling, criticisms of Alistair Darling and the seemingly boundless energy of the Yes campaign, is it time to worry about Better Together? Yes and no. Nicola Sturgeon has spent a large chunk of her political career preparing herself for this campaign, she's an aggressive debater and will know the White Paper inside out and back to front. In comparison Alistair Carmichael is a relative newcomer to the front line of the debate. Given the circumstances I think escaping with all his limbs still attached is enough to be going on with. Fortunately the influence of a single brief TV debate during a current affairs show isn't likely to have much bearing on the outcome of the referendum.

As someone who would never consider voting for him, I'd have to say that Alistair Darling has been doing a perfectly acceptable job. He wasn't given the job because of an ability to bounce around the TV studios like Tigger in a Union Jack. He's there to be calm and measured as he pours cold water over the nationalists' latest assertion or un-costed promise. Raw passion for your beliefs is worthless if you aren't capable of talking about the complex detail with authority. Anyone who is unconvinced should watch Eddi Reader's contribution to the recent *BBC Question Time* from Falkirk.

Both Yes Scotland and Better Together are not without their flaws and weaknesses. Part of the problem is that because of the phenomenal length of this debate, our concept of time has become warped. It's still possible to conceive and give birth to a child before the date of the referendum so it's not ridiculous for the campaigns to be pacing themselves even now. Moving into 2014, Better Together will perhaps have to spend less time purely countering Yes Scotland and make more of the arguments for the UK.

Better Together still has the lead in the polls, although how large that lead is depends significantly on which polling company you listen to. It's clear that the first instinct of the majority is to vote no to independence. "Scotland's Future" is part of an effort by the Yes campaign to give credibility to independence thereby making it a more acceptable proposition. There are two distinct strands of argument for Better Together to use. The arguments for the UK and the arguments against independence. Until now, the focus has very much been on the latter. As the onslaught from Yes Scotland ramps up, it becomes more important to remind people why they want to stay in the UK. As strange as it might sound, the best bet for Better Together might be to take a step back from some of the day to day politics. The three pro-UK parties will all lay out their own ideas for Scotland's future in the UK. It's up to Better Together to remind voters that the UK is more than just politics and economics.

Harold Macmillan wrote a note for his Downing Street office which read "Quiet, calm deliberation disentangles every knot". Politics is a battle, matching your opponent blow for blow and fighting fire with fire; but it's also a chess game, it's about strategy and choosing your battles. Taking the time to give a considered response shouldn't be mistaken for inactivity or a lack of ability. It's always a good idea to look before you leap because as President Kennedy said "All men can fly, but sadly only in one direction." A fact we should all remember, perhaps particularly unnamed senior Tories.

Would independence be a supermarket sweep?

Brian Monteith
14 December 2013

The Yes Scotland campaign ran into serious trouble this week – and it came from a most unlikely quarter – supermarkets.

The SNP's White Paper becomes more irrelevant with every 24 hours that passes as the cold light of each day reminds us that what's on offer is a nothing other than a fantastical wish-list thought up by politicians that repeatedly fail to deliver on their promises. It's the longest letter to Santa ever written, but somebody forgot to tell Alex Salmond and Nicola Sturgeon he's a figure of make believe. In real life if you want to get that train set, extra pocket money and doctors and nurses outfits you have to earn them. It's called hard work.

Just this week we heard how the SNP's pledge on smaller class sizes has still not been delivered – six years on. Remember, this is a pledge that the Scottish government has complete control over; it cannot blame David Cameron, Climate Change or the *wrong type of snow*.

There is an honourable case for independence and it's a very simple one. It does not take 670 expensive pages, a direct mail campaign to every elector in the land and a roadshow in town

57

halls (with curries all round afterwards) to communicate it. The case is that Scotland should decide everything for itself, that it should not share its sovereignty with other nations. It will not be a land of milk and honey, but it will be a place where we have taken responsibility for our choices, can look in the mirror and live with ourselves – not blaming the Americans (for warmongering), Europeans (for depleting our fish) or the English (for practically everything else).

Scots will not stop moaning, for we will have to learn to moan at ourselves and stop blaming others.

It is because too many politicians like to pass the buck that the SNP offers independence *without* independence; I mean not being in the UK but still using its currency; saying we will take 100,000 more immigrants (*it's in the White Paper*) but pretending the English won't put border posts up as a result; or having different taxes and regulations but expecting businesses to behave as if we are still one British market.

So it was refreshing that the top four British supermarkets let it be known this week, through the *Financial Times*, that Scotland could face higher grocery prices if we become a foreign country.

The obvious question is why has it taken them so long to speak up? The answer of course was provided in the response of the SNP, Yes Campaign and their followers. The story was rubbished as "scaremongering", some nationalists called for a boycott of the stores and the Director of Communities at Yes Scotland tweeted that it would be good if Tesco were to leave Scotland. (This is not an isolated view, there are many who would love to turn an independent Scotland into a Socialist nirvana where, you will be lucky if there's anything other than cabbages on the shelves. I visited East Germany and the Soviet Union and that was the reality for housewives doing the shopping).

Of course supermarkets might have to charge more, they already carry the extra costs that devolution has brought of over £30 million, but currently takes that on the chin as the economics of operating a separate pricing regime would not recoup the extra income. But if Scotland were to be independent, with separate food and employment regulations, different taxation to process (would VAT remain the same? It's 25% in Denmark) then the point could come when it suddenly makes sense to pass extra costs on to Scottish customers – especially if it allowed the supermarkets to cut their prices in the united English and Welsh single market that would be ten times the size.

The SNP tried to argue that lower corporation tax and lower fuel duty would encourage Scottish food prices to go down, but lower business taxes would not operate in isolation, but carry their own regulatory burden that would have to far outweigh the separate bureaucracy costs. More problematic still is that during the SNP's six years of power large companies like supermarkets have seen the burden of taxation go up – and the regulations blossom – while in England they have fallen in both respects.

What this little skirmish tells us is that there examples where we can share the costs and risks across the whole of Britain – to our benefit. Warnings that we might not like the change have to be put before we decide. This is not scaremongering it is pointing out the positives that already exist and the negatives of taking them away.

The problem for the No campaign is that people don't always know what they have until they lose it – and by then it can be too late. With a referendum from which there will be no going back it is vital that businesses tell us what the implications are on our lives, their products and services, the jobs they provide and the investment they make.

Whether they support a Yes or a No, businesses need to be heard without fear of intimidation.

The great myth of UK inequality

Murdo Fraser
14 December 2013

IT HAS BECOME something of a statement of faith for the "Yes campaign" to break up Britain that the UK is one of the most unequal countries in the world. This is a claim often repeated by Yes campaigners in the media. One can hardly watch a TV debate on independence without someone, either from the panel or the audience, referring to this supposed "fact".

The Yes Scotland website states "the UK is the fourth most unequal country in the developed world". This claim was repeated in the parliamentary chamber as recently as Wednesday of this week by SNP MSP Joan McAlpine, who stated "the United Kingdom is the fourth most unequal country in the developed world".

The SNP White Paper on independence, "Scotland's Future", states something slightly different: "The UK ranks 28th out of 34 nations in the OECD on a measure of overall equality". (p.44). This is reiterated at various points, for example p. 135 "the UK is already one of the developed world's most unequal societies".

This supposed inequality in UK society is held up as a primary reason for separation of Scotland from the UK although, interestingly, it is quite hard to find the argument as to why an independent Scotland would necessarily be any different.

How much validity is there in these (conflicting) claims? Are we the 4th most unequal country in the developed world, as Yes Scotland and sundry SNP MSPs would claim, or the 6th, as stated in the White Paper? Or is the reality something entirely different? I thought I should try and find out.

Inequality is measured by what is known as the "Gini coefficient"[1], drawn up by the United Nations, the World Bank, the US CIA, and the OECD. The Gini coefficient is a number between zero and one, where zero corresponds with perfect equality (where everyone has the same income) and one corresponds with perfect inequality (where one person has all the income – and everyone else has zero income). So the lower the GINI coefficient, the more equal the society.

For the purpose of the exercise, let us assume that equality of outcomes is what matters, and that greater equality is desirable. Many would argue, however, that what matters is equality of opportunity, but let us lay that aside for the moment. Let us also assume that the data collected on income and wealth, derived from household surveys, is comparable across countries, which may not necessarily be the case.

What the data tells us is that the Gini coefficient for the UK for income, after transfers and taxes are applied, is calculated at 0.345. By comparison, Denmark is 0.240, Sweden 0.250, Norway 0.258, Germany 0.283 and France 0.327. Across the world, this puts the UK rank in terms of inequality at 43 out of 156 countries, well within the top third of the most equal societies. Ah, but, Nationalists will claim, the comparison is with the developed world, in other words the OECD countries (although this distinction is not always made by Yes campaigners). Here they appear to be closer to the truth. The UK ranks 28th out of 34 in terms of the Gini coefficient, the 6th most unequal, not the 4th. So even on this measurement Yes Scotland (and Joan McAlpine) are in error.

But this is not the full picture.

Income only represents part of the story. Perhaps more important is the distribution of wealth in society, and here the data tells us something quite different. In the recently-published Global Wealth Databook 2013 produced by Credit Suisse (published October 2013)[2], the UK Gini coefficient for wealth distribution is assessed (in percentage terms) as 67.7. That puts the UK at 14 out of 34 OECD countries, comfortably in the upper half.

France (69.0), Germany (77.1) and Switzerland (80.6) are all below us (i.e. more unequal societies).

Still more interesting is the placing of Scandinavian countries. Finland is at 66.1 and Iceland 67.3, marginally more equal than the UK. But Norway (77.8), Sweden (80.3) and Denmark, the land of Borgen, (107.7) are all less equal than the UK.

This is such a remarkable finding it is worth highlighting. For years the Scandinavian countries have been held up by the SNP and their fellow travellers on the left as models of the socially-just and equal economies which an independent Scotland should aspire to emulate. But in terms of distribution of wealth, the data is clear: *Norway, Sweden and Denmark are all less equal than the UK.*

The consequence of this is that a vote for independence in order to leave the UK and be more like Scandinavia is a vote not, as nationalists would claim, for a more equal society, but for precisely the opposite. And it means that both Yes Scotland, and the SNP, are deliberately trying to mislead the public about the current political situation in the UK for their own partisan purposes. Will Yes Scotland be changing their website? Will the SNP be amending their White Paper? If they had any integrity, they would be doing so now.

---

[1] http://en.wikipedia.org/wiki/List_of_countries_by_income_equality
[2] https://publications.credit-suisse.com/tasks/render/file/?fileID=1949208D-E59A-F2D9-6D0361266E44A2F8

Energy remains a blind spot for nationalists

Neil Craig
16 December 2013

THE ENTIRE energy question is covered in Chapter 8 of the White Paper entitled "Environment, Rural Affairs, Energy and Resources" which reflects the degree of priority given to energy, despite the fact that energy use is pretty much identical to GDP.

ELECTRICITY
The boast "Between January 2010 and April 2013, industry has announced £13.1 billion of investment with an associated 9,100 jobs". That, at £1.44 million per job would not be that wonderful even if Verso Economics had not previously proven that for every "Green" job created 3.7 jobs in the non-subsidised economy are destroyed. Add the decision of Scottish Power to pull out of its previously announced intention to invest in a Hebridean windfarm, and many other recent cancellations of windmill projects and even that promise looks improbable.

In fact none of this £13.1 billion would have been on offer were it not that wind energy is getting a 200 per cent subsidy. The Scottish government has not only already promised we will be 100 per cent renewable by 2020 but every major conventional power generator is intended to close before 2020 except:

65

• *Longannet*: coal, 2.4 GW, opened 1972, the station is expected to continue operating until approximately 2020-2025, because of the technical advancements in place at the station. These include the station's low NOx burners and its NOx reburn system

• *Hunterston* B: nuclear, 1.288 GW, opened 1976, Hunterston B was originally planned to operate until 2011. In 2007 planned operation was extended by 5 years to 2016. In December 2012 EDF said it could (technically and economically) operate until 2023.

• *Torness*: nuclear, 1.344 GW, opened 1988, it is expected to operate until 2023

• *Peterhead*; gas, was 1550GW, opened 1980, 660 megawatt Peterhead Unit Two likely to close taking Peterhead transmission capacity down to 1,180 megawatts – undated but clearly current. Peterhead has also not got the Westminster £1bn subsidy for carbon capture that Holyrood wanted and was listed by Jim McDonald as due to close before 2030.

We are building no new large capacity generators. We will soon have none. Windmills simply cannot provide baseload because they are intermittent, even the government funded lobbyists, Scottish Renewables accept this. So how will the power be kept on?

Despite the 100 per cent renewable promise the White Paper promises incentives to provide "renewable and thermal", which looks like two incompatible promises but I am assured there is an explanation. The big question is how Scotland can afford to be 100 per cent renewable when everybody accepts wind is more expensive. Particularly when we are assured not only that Holyrood will oppose fuel poverty but that they will have a statutory duty to end fuel poverty.

This is how:

"This Government proposes that a single Transmission Operator will continue to balance supply and demand across Scotland and the rest of the UK.

Following independence, Scottish renewable energy will continue to represent the most cost-effective means for the rest of the UK to meet its renewable ambitions. The continuation of a system of shared support for renewables and capital costs of transmission among consumers in Scotland and the rest of the UK is a reasonable consideration for meeting the UK's ongoing green commitments. "

The rest of the UK will continue to subsidise our windmills.

Nationalist politicians are honest enough to say that this is simply what the SNP "proposes" but it is clearly insane. Nobody can guarantee that England will continue to elect governments willing to pour subsidies into a foreign country. But having admitted it is only a proposal there is no plan B should the English electorate decide otherwise.

Bear in mind that Ofgen have already said they expect electricity bills to rise to £3,000 a year across the UK by 2020 when the UK will not yet have reached its target of 30 per cent renewable. Scotland's 100 per cent target would, on our own, clearly be well beyond impossible without English subsidy. Ignoring the question shows the SNP to be unfit to hold any responsible job.

Actually its worse than that – because wind is intermittent, and particularly likely to be missing when it is cold, we will would need English help to keep the lights on in any case and irrespective of cost. Indeed either way we will need to strengthen the cross border interconnector either to sell as much of our spare windpower as promised or to bring in enough English conventional power at need.

The paper also guarantees that £70 per household of the energy levies will be transferred to tax. With 2 million Scots households and 2/3 of power use being non-domestic that comes to £420 million – 1.3p on income tax or some equivalent – both unspecified. This and other spending promises for an independent country look to be adding about 20p to income taxes or equivalent. I await hearing of their equivalent.

OIL & GAS

The long prophesied Oil Fund gets another mention but since no promise of how much will go into it, or when, it may safely be ignored. Good thing, since that money is currently being spent.

I found this interesting remark about gas "Scotland is also estimated to have the second largest volume of proven gas reserves in the EU after the Netherlands". The key word being "proven" which allows the authors to ignore shale gas though it is orders of magnitude more than conventional gas and the UK may be the European leader. Most shale is in northern England but there is enough under Scotland's central belt that, per capita, a separate Scotland would not lose out. Or at least would not lose out unless we decided to. But the SNP has promised ever more regulation to prevent it being produced.

Grangemouth was saved because the owner decided to bring in US shale gas (which costs 1/3rd of what ours does) to process, but this is like carrying coals to Newcastle in that we could be getting this gas from Fife.

Another interesting omission is under Decommissioning. This is about getting England to pay for decommissioning of oil rigs. The omission is any mention of decommissioning nuclear plants, Over the decades the government have taken over £40 billion from the nuclear industry to be held by them in a "decommissioning fund" – in fact no such fund exists or it would, accounting for inflation and interest, now be worth well above £200 billion. It is out of character that they don't stake a claim to a disproportionate share of this and I think it is evidence of their blank spot over nuclear rather than any goodwill.

I am not trying to say that Scotland cannot afford separation. A Scotland favourable to economic freedom, willing to allow us to have shale gas and nuclear power at a market price would undoubtedly be far wealthier than the current UK. Hinkley Point is to cost four times more than an equivalent European-built project in China – and almost equally important for investor returns, will take 10 years rather than 3 to complete, entirely due to government parasitism.

Which brings me to my last extract from the paper:

"If we form the government of an independent Scotland we will:

seek to enshrine environmental protection in the constitution. With independence we will have the opportunity to enshrine protection of our environment in the proposed written constitution for Scotland"

I'm of the old fashioned view that the purpose of a constitution is to limit the power the state has over us, rather than the EU style one, that it is to give judges and those in power more power over us and limit our power to object. The White Paper's approach is very much of the latter sort. It says what government can do and even what we cannot object to the state doing. No wording is given but there is difficulty in concluding that it would say, or after a few years interpretation would be deemed to say, that we mortals have no right to object to anything the ecofascists claim is necessary.

Ultimately even that nobody not willing to claim to see catastrophic warming (or whatever the next eco-scare is) at every hand, could stand for election. Holyrood voted for the world's most restrictive Climate Change Act and did so with Soviet style unanimity – how many of those MSPs would object to it being enshrined in the constitution to keep future generations restrained too?

The strange case of the dog that never barked

Brian Monteith
16 December 2013

It is one of the strange aspects to the debate about Scottish independence that neither the Better Together campaign nor the three main unionist parties mention the Scotland Act 2012.

It is argued, for I have seen it put by all sides, that it is an irrelevance because it has been overtaken by events. In some respects political developments have indeed passed it by; the Liberal Democrats have published a report saying how they would like to go much further while the Labour and Conservative parties will do so in Spring – and anyway there's the referendum on independence in September.

There are no political leaders with any clout in Scotland that expound the view that the latest Scotland Act will be the last for some time, even Ruth Davidson has allowed her line in the sand to be washed away Canute-like by the tide of realpolitik. Nevertheless the debate about what will happen to Scotland if we reject independence is conducted as if how we are governed now will remain the status quo when all politicians know that the arrangements will change in 2015.

This unavoidable fact might be considered an inconvenient

truth for nationalists, for the new arrangements could reveal two realities for the unionists to point to.

The first is that the Scotland Act gives testimony to the credibility of the unionist parties that they can be trusted to bring forward changes to devolution that gives more power over taxation to the benefit of the Scottish Parliament. This credibility is especially robust because the legislation was introduced and passed by a Conservative-led coalition government following a cross-party process that evolved from a Labour Party policy initiative.

If the unionist parties continue to argue that they will give further powers to Holyrood then their record suggests they can be trusted on the matter. Indeed it was the SNP that initially put the process in jeopardy and eventually backed down – rather like it first did with the constitutional convention all those years ago that delivered the Holyrood parliament in the first place.

The second point is that it will be the SNP, and especially John Swinney, that shall have to bring forward financial proposals applying the new powers that the Scotland Act gives to vary existing and new taxes. The SNP is very keen to tell the public what it will do with independence – spending hundreds of thousands of taxpayers' pounds on a White paper, accompanying junk mail and Radio Salmond Roadshow for a constitutional policy that remains a minority pursuit – but has thus far told us hee-haw about how it will approach the financial implications of legislation that is now on the statute.

Where are the projections, the option papers, the questions and answers and the call to arms that the new powers will be used to make Scotland more equal, more egalitarian, more Scandinavian, *ad infinitum*? Or are we to believe that in the same way the SNP does not utilise the current powers to vary a number of existing taxes it has no intention to change anything?

Just as the SNP has already shown it is scared to make Scottish independence seem too different from Scotland remaining part of the UK – by keeping the pound, the monarchy, the NATO membership, the Bank of England oversight, the university research funding, the open borders, amongst others – it appears the SNP is also scared to make devolution any different too.

These are points that I am surprised the No campaign has not yet raised, it is as if the Scotland Act is the dog that does not bark, that it has been muzzled by its owners.

I mention this because there is a great disappointment amongst many committed activists of either persuasion and by interested spectators of the debate that the White Paper has not been the game changer that was hoped. Rather than be the inspirational document it could and should have been it is the longest wish list ever composed in time for Santa Claus, an imaginary figure that will not get down Bute House Chimney.

Journalists are now being briefed by the Yes campaign that three events next year will make up for this disappointment and provide a swing towards Salmond and his campaign. It is said that the European elections will make Europhile Scotland look more different from a Eurosceptic England, that the growing possibility of a Conservative re-election in the 2015 general election will scare Scottish voters, and that the Labour and Conservative parties' reports into further powers will come up short and be unsatisfactory to voters. It is argued all of these developments will push more Scots towards a Yes and be, individually or together, the much needed game changer.

It does not take a sharp political analyst to notice that all three of these arguments are highly negative; scaremongering you might call it. It is as if the utopian promises of the White Paper never happened.

It is also noticeable that such optimistic hopes over experience take no account of opinion polling showing Ukip could do well in Scotland in next June's elections, or that the odds are so stacked in favour of Labour being returned to office that the best David Cameron can hope for is another coalition agreement with the

Liberal Democrats. That Nick Clegg may not even be elected again and leadership of the Liberal Democrats could fall to someone else such as Labour-leaning Vince Cable appears not to have been factored in.

That the likelihood is either a coalition or Labour government is a prospect at Westminster is an important factor – for the total voter numbers, vote share and MPs of the Liberal Democrat and Conservative parties in Scotland, or Labour by itself, were both greater than the combined performance of the SNP and Green parties in 2010 – and could be so again.

Then on the final possibility – that the offer of greater powers cannot be believed – all unionist parties can point to the Devolution Act and say they can be trusted to deliver. SNP complaints about a reduced or abolished Barnett Formula are beside the point, the reason behind greater powers is for Scottish politicians to take as much responsibility for their spending as possible. As with independence, further devolution means the Barnet Formula as we know it must go.

The status quo must change. It is time the No campaign took the muzzle off and let its dog bark – and bite. Release the hounds!

Does local government have a future in 'Scotland's Future'?

David Meikle
17 December 2013

I FINALLY got my hands on it this week. It's what everyone in Scotland is talking about. I am, of course, referring to "Scotland's Future", the SNP Government's White Paper on independence.

At 670 pages it isn't exactly a light read but is visually stunning with striking photographs and infographics. What's most important, however, is not the length or how attractive it is but the content; so what about that? Inevitably, as a councillor I was immediately drawn to search the document for any content on local government.

As a Scottish Conservative, I believe in localism and devolving more powers to councils and communities as much as possible. So what does this weighty, glossy document say about local government in an independent Scotland and would this localism agenda be furthered if Scotland voted 'Yes' in 2014?

To be fair, the White Paper (or *#indyplan* as it's known on twitter) does have a bit to say about local government. It has two specific sections relating to it: on pages 366 to 368 – while on pages 576 to 579 there is a question and answer session on council issues.

But before I go on to look at both sections in detail, I think it is worth pointing out that local government is already devolved to Scotland. The Scottish Government could, if it wants, change local authority boundaries and scrap the Council Tax. In fact under devolution there have been major changes to local government: the introduction of a new electoral system; the creation of large, multi-member wards; councillors receiving a salary; the Council Tax freeze; and with the creation of the national Fire and Police services we saw the removal of responsibilities from Councils.

Given these substantial changes, what is it that independence could do for local government that already can't be done under the current constitutional set up we have in Scotland?

The first (and main) section in the document on local government is found in part 4, chapter 10 of the White Paper. It forms part of what the SNP is calling "Building a Modern Democracy".

The repetitive narrative and a key selling point of independence is "democracy" seemingly ignorant that Scotland has a Scottish Parliament with a range of powers including over local government but let's leave that to one side. In a nutshell the SNP believes that with independence there is a "new opportunity to consider the right level for decisions to be made".

The SNP government believes it has shown a good working relationship between it and local government that can blossom under independence. The irony is that this relationship has developed under the current constitutional set up and any Scottish government has the power to devolve powers to local government – you don't need independence to do either of these things. This section also focuses on the work currently being undertaken to develop the Islands' communities and the Cities Alliance; work it is able to do under the current constitutional set up. The only new thing I can see is it says with independence we can implement the European Charter on Local Self-Government.

The second part of the White Paper on local government is the question and answer section. It is very useful and I'm sure members of the public will find it easy to use. The section on local government repeats much of what is said in part 10, chapter 4 i.e. that local government will be an integral part of good governance of Scotland. It reiterates the current Council Tax system, funding arrangements will continue on independence. It also says the same services will be delivered by Councils as they are now using the same local authority boundaries.

On business rates it seems from the White Paper the SNP government plans to continue with the attractive arrangements now in place in Scotland (thanks of course to the Scottish Conservatives for delivering this!)

All in all a bit of a mixed bag on local government but what about the rest of the document: does it have anything to say on it? I came across a helpful diagram on page 39 on how Scotland will be governed if we vote 'Yes'. What's missing from it is any detail of the structure below the Scottish Parliament and Government. Is this a deliberate omission? Maybe not because on page 47 the White Paper says:

"On independence, the structure of local government in Scotland will remain the same, with local councils continuing to deliver the full range of services they do today. This will include schools, leisure and social services. The next election to Scotland's local authorities will take place as planned in 2017."

Taking this into account I'm left scratching my head to figure out what we gain with independence. Essentially the main 'Yes' argument on local government is about enshrining it in a written constitution. For example "Scotland's Future" says:

"Independence will give us the power to embed the role of local authorities in a written constitution and consider the most

appropriate responsibilities for local government and communities."

Put simply the document says a 'Yes' vote will not immediately change the structure of 32 councils in Scotland but as part of the constitutional convention (i.e. the creation of a constitution for an independent Scotland) the role, responsible and powers of councils will be discussed and debated then. In other words it is up to the convention to decide on the status, rights, responsibilities, boundaries and so on of local government.

Is there any indication of where the SNP would stand in this debate? Only two points caught my eye. On page 332 one of the main bullet points says "We will support greater subsidiarity and local decision-making". That sounds interesting but there's not a lot of beef, e.g. what about devolving more tax-raising powers to Councils or different funding arrangements? There is a lame statement on the government believing local government should have the power to decide what is best for local people but that's it.

The second point is on page 577 where it says: "the current council tax system is unfair…and will consult with other to develop options for a fairer and more progressive local tax". Could this mean the return of the misnomer *local income tax* the SNP has proposed previously but failed to deliver on, despite now having the majority in the Parliament to do so? This is not clear.

In summary, what the White Paper offers on local government is no immediate change; local government being part of the new constitution; and in the future maybe some change on council tax and councils' responsibilities. What can be ascertained is that local government will have a future in an independent Scotland, but beyond the current parameters there is little illumination on what a different future looks like.

The UK is not so unequal, and becoming less so

Murdo Fraser
21 December 2013

IT IS ONE of life's great ironies that the "Yes campaign" to break up Britain constantly complains about the "negativity" of the Better Together campaign. It is itself, of course, relentlessly negative towards the United Kingdom, and this negativity extends to misrepresenting the current state of the UK economy and society.

Last week in this column I challenged the Yes campaign statement that "the UK is the fourth most unequal country in the developed world". If the reaction on Twitter is anything to go by, this slaying of the separatists' sacred cow left them howling at the moon in fury.

The principal reaction from Nationalists seemed to be one of simple disbelief. "We cannot be unfairer than that lovely cuddly Scandinavian nirvana," came the shrieks, "it's simply impossible".

To use a seasonal analogy, it is a bit like the small child discovering Santa really does not exist, that it is just his Dad who has delivered the presents, knocked back the sherry, and scoffed the mince pie, and having a screaming tantrum and shouting "It's not true!" whilst stamping his feet on the floor.

And yet the data is there in black and white, and I have yet to see any serious attempt to challenge it. Some drew attention to the contrast in Gini co-efficient between the OECD figures and those in the Credit Suisse Global Wealth Databook 2013, but completely missed the point that these are measurements of two different matters – income, and wealth.

Now it is clear that there is a variation in the data between the two measurements. In terms of income inequality the UK is ranked at 28th out of 34 OECD countries, whilst for wealth we are ranked at 14th. But nowhere does the data support the Yes campaign's claim of "fourth most unequal country in the developed world".

Let anyone think I am alone in drawing these conclusions, I would point to the excellent blogs[1] by John Rentoul of the Independent, hardly a Conservative commentator, who has himself stated that the facts are "hard to believe", but are. facts nonetheless.

Rentoul highlights another unexpected finding, one which will ruin Christmas even more for blinkered Nationalists. For not only is the claim that we are one of the most unequal countries in the developed world unsupported by the evidence (as we have established), but so is the claim that inequality in the UK has been growing.

The Yes Scotland website states "income inequality has increased over the past decades". But has it?

The independent Office of National Statistics, in its "The Effect of Taxes and Benefits on Household Income" report published in July 2013, states that inequality (of income)[2] in the UK is at its lowest level since 1986. The Institute for Fiscal Studies uses a slightly different set of statistics[3], but the underlying message is essentially the same. It shows that inequality increased during the 1980s, was then broadly flat for two decades, and has fallen slightly since 2010. The latest figure is comparable to 1990. Even if we look at figures for income after housing costs, there has been a recent reduction in inequality which means we are now no more unequal than we were in 2005-06.

Whichever study is used, there is a consistent message of inequality having reduced in the UK over at least the last decade or so, and certainly since 2010 when the last Labour government lost power. So the current Coalition government, far from increasing income inequality as is often claimed, has in fact reduced it.

None of this will make comfortable reading for Nationalists. Cue outrage and bluster on social media. But, as the First Minister is fond of saying: "Facts are chiels that winna ding".

[1] http://blogs.independent.co.uk/2013/11/06/cameron-on-inequality/
[2] http://www.ons.gov.uk/ons/dcp171778_317365.pdf
[3] http://www.ifs.org.uk/pr/inequality_recession_june2013.pdf

France tells us we should be careful what we wish for

Brian Monteith
3 January 2014

Last week I wondered if 2014 would bring anything different for us from our politicians. I came to a rather lamentable conclusion, born of much experience, that even if some things changed everything would remain the same.

Despite this I remain an optimist. My glass is always half full- to brimming over, for I believe in the ability of humankind to overcome adversity through a blend of creativity, ingenuity and indomitable perseverance. So this week I thought I would write about how change is indeed possible – but with a warning for those that think the grass is always greener on the other side I suggest we should always be careful about what we wish for.

This year I spent Hogmanay in France. We had a great party seeing in the New Year; for a little while the corner of Gaul that we occupied became a part of Caledonia. Our house was decked with saltires, the tartans of our guests hung as pennants from the rafters and my wife and I laid on a Scottish feast.

I had made my own haggis from the pluck of a French Lamb

and some imported Scottish oatmeal and suet. You could call it a new twist on the Auld Alliance. My wife Jackie baked a super Clootie dumpling and Black Bun, and together we made some whisky cocktails to get our guests in the mood. For entertainment we laid on some Scottish Country Dancing between a playlist of Scottish bands from Average White Band to Stone the Crows to Wet, Wet, Wet. Our English visitors entered into the spirit with some creative use of tartan attire and we gave them some Edinburgh rock as a little thank you.

The television was not switched on until the afternoon of second of January.

Being the only Scots present, Jackie and I were often asked what we expect to happen in the referendum. Our answer is simple and undeviating, if a little tongue-in-cheek for English ears, that Scots would be daft to settle for running only Scotland when we have the opportunity to run the whole of Britain. Inside the UK Scotland punches above its weight and while we may not always get what we want we often direct British institutions from the front or from behind the scenes – be it government, the civil service (especially the Foreign Office), the BBC and all sorts of British companies, charities, sports bodies, cultural organisations and the media.

I have travelled a lot and over the last seven years I have worked a good deal overseas; what I have witnessed is the significant presence Scots have as players in business, industry and government through British channels of influence. What I also believe – and have seen – is that nationalism has a corrosive side to it that has to be restrained; it is one thing to be proud of one's country's successes but there has to be humility too. Be it British or Scottish (or, say, Chinese or American) nationalism it has to be kept in check.

In France the mood is now rather sullen. After the Presidential elections of 2012 there was great hope that the new socialist President Francois Hollande would be the answer to the nation's problems. His mantra sounds rather similar to that coming fom those advocating a Brave New Scotland; Hollande would reject economic austerity as the solution to a debt-fuelled recession, he would employ more public servants funded by the taxpayer and he would fund this and achieve greater equality by raising the taxes on the the rich.

That's pretty much what the SNP's White Paper argued for – greater public spending on a long wish list of things our parents never had but we are told we cannot live without; a convenient oversight that Scotland (and, by the way, also Britain) continues to spend beyond its means – requiring the freedom to tax more and to fill the gap; with the narrative that the new free services and taxes on the rich will make us more equal than the rest of Britain.

French socialism, like Scottish nationalism, is a direct challenge to the austerity policies of London and Berlin. Free at last, we will be able to beat our chests and say "whae's like us".

Well, certainly not the French, for there the dreams have quickly turned sour. French unemployment has hit a sixteen year high at 11 per cent and nearly a million more than the UK where we have record levels of employment and the jobless rate of 7.4 per cent is the lowest since 2009. Emigration is in vogue; the number of French now working in Britain has climbed by 25% since 2010 and London is the sixth largest "French City".

So poor is the French economy – that Moody's has downgraded the French credit rating for the second time in two years – and with Hollande's approval rating the lowest of any President since the beginning of the Fifth Republic in 1958 – that a new programme of tax and spending cuts has been announced.

Somebody once said things can only get better, but the truth is things can also get worse. We should always be careful about what we wish for.

The SNP's callous disregard for children and parents

Brian Monteith
7 January 2014

THE SNP has made the cause of better childcare in Scotland one of the core attractions of its appeal to voters in this year's independence referendum – and yet the party has shown by its own actions in government that it has nothing but a callous disregard for the plight of young children and their parents.

A highly partisan opinion? Then read on and consider the SNP's actions and motives.

When the White Paper was announced a policy of improved free childcare was announced that was clearly aimed at attracting women voters to the independence cause, a group that polling shows is far more sceptical than males of comparable ages. Critics immediately pounced on the idea, pointing out that the Scottish Parliament already has the necessary powers to be able to direct funds and alter legislation to provide the free childcare policy.

The SNP defence is simple enough – and was repeated in last weekend's *Scotland on Sunday* by the First Minister Alex Salmond – that the Scottish Government could not afford to introduce the policy because it would be paid for by the savings made on reduced welfare payments and the additional revenues from increased income tax contributions as more parents, predominantly women, enter the workplace. These financial benefits would accrue to the Westminster Treasury and would not feed in to the funding available to the Scottish Financial Secretary, John Swinney.

This argument is disingenuous, and here's why.

Firstly, if the policy is attractive because it is right for children to have access to early years education and right for their parents to go to work and improve the living standards of the family (not to say right for the Scottish economy that might want to access the available skills) then it should be supported because of its intrinsic value in Scotland irrespective of financial benefits that might accrue to the UK Treasury. Introduction of the policy therefore comes down to a matter of political will – that is the willingness of the SNP to find the necessary savings to effect a policy that is clearly popular and widely supported and that it has the power to deliver.

Avoiding the application of the policy on the basis of the need for independence beforehand suggests a callous disregard for the merits and benefits of the policy – at the expense of trying to foment a grievance that might build electoral support. It is putting party advantage before people and party advantage before country.

Secondly, even if the financial benefits would accrue to a Scottish Government rather than a Westminster one there would be a time lag of at least a year (probably longer, tapering over two to three years) as the take-up by parents kicked in and the savings followed afterwards. In other words the Scottish Government would have to find the finances *in advance* of the policy and would therefore have to take tough decisions at least two years before its introduction (to account for financial budgeting). Yet what we see now is the complete avoidance of any willingness to take tough decisions before a referendum lest it effect the outcome. Where would the savings be made? Silence from the SNP. How would the time-lag be funded? Er, hmm, yet more silence.

Thirdly, the SNP's defence also ignores two alternative approaches; the first is that independence is not a prerequisite for obtaining the financial benefits because an improved form of devolution could be delivered (and might yet be in the offing from the unionist parties) that would provide the same financial savings and increased revenues that the SNP bemoans it will not see; the second is that it rules out what would be a perfectly reasonable approach by the Scottish Financial Secretary to open up negotiations with the UK Treasury to realise a share of such financial benefits *pro tem*. By following either or both strategies (they are not mutually exclusive) there is no need for a Scottish Government to present such a black and white contrast of the status quo with no improved childcare versus independence that would deliver it.

The conclusion must be that the SNP presents the policy this way purely for electoral advantage – betraying its callous disregard for children and parents. Even if you give the benefit of the doubt to the SNP at this stage of reasoning, believing that the budgeting difficulties might be insurmountable, the record of the SNP Government tells us that it is simply not interested in using the powers at its disposal and the funds available to it to help children and parents with early years provision.

The simple fact is that children in Scotland are not all treated equally by the SNP government and that thus far the SNP ministers have steadfastly refused to change the system so that no child will be left behind.

As the think tank Reform Scotland has previously highlighted, currently only fifty per cent of children born in Scotland are entitled to two years' provision due to the way the SNP government's rules are applied.

The reason for this is that in Scotland a child's entitlement to government-funded nursery provision starts the term *after* a child turns three. As a result, a child born between 1 March and 31 August would be entitled to the full two years' nursery provision before beginning school. A child born between 1 September 1 and 31 December would, however, only receive 18 months and a child born between 1 January and 28 February would get just 15 months.

Amendments to the Scottish Government's Children and Young People (Scotland) Bill are currently being considered by the Education & Culture committee. During the stage 1 debate, MSPs from Labour, the Conservatives and the Liberal Democrats all indicated that they wanted all children to be given the same basic provision. So far the scottish Government has resisted such a change and to bring the matter to a head the Conservative member, Liz Smith has brought forward amendments to the Bill that would bring about equality.

Smith has commented, "Discrimination within nursery provision as a result of the date of a child's birthday is completely unacceptable. The difference can vary by up to 317 hours or by more than £1,000 within the cost of partnership nursery provision."

If the Scottish Government votes the amendments down it will be showing that even when it has the powers and the funds to deliver change it is not interested. It will be showing a callous disregard for children who are treated unequally by its own regulations – nothing to do with Westminster and nothing to do with the UK Treasury.

Alison Payne of Reform Scotland has explained the argument succinctly, "Just as all children are entitled to seven years of primary education irrespective of their date of birth, they should be entitled to a basic two years of government-funded nursery provision. To achieve this, Reform Scotland believes that nursery provision should start at a fixed point in the year, probably in August, just as it does for school."

If the SNP cannot bring itself to deliver equality from the current early years public service provision now, why should its sincerity be believed for policies in the future?

The sad fact is that the party is hoist by its own petard. It hoped to seduce voters, especially women, to the cause of independence with a blatant bribe that only a few parents would have the knowledge through experience to question. Once challenged it has avoided the fact that it could, if it wanted, deliver the policy already – and that where it does preside over such policy it is so far unwilling to deliver it equitably for all children.

A callous disregard for parents and children? It cannot be called anything else unless you are the most loyal, obedient and partisan supporter of the SNP.

Scottish citizenship will become no more than an SNP residency test

Jonathan Stanley
8 January 2014

THE SNP is planning to abolish a separate Scottish citizenship by remaining in the EU. The following is my opinion based on two outcomes. The first is both Scotland and the rest of the UK both remain in the EU, the second that Scotland leaves the EU and has at least an *interregnum* period where we will be in accession but not a member.

Scotland inside the EU
If Scotland is allowed to continue as an EU member Scotland will automatically remain within the European Economic Area (EEA). Freedom of movement and free access to most emergency health care are EEA competences and freedom of employment and social security are EU competences.

We cannot answer the question of Scottish citizenship fully until the Scottish Government releases its legal advice to corroborate claims made that we would remain inside the EU post-2016 as a separate state. This would require a universal approval of current member states and would essentially excuse

Scotland from accession criteria and negotiation. This would have to be agreed; else the default position is we would be OUT.

Any British citizen and any new citizen born inside the EU would remain or have right to become an EU citizen. This will mean they would have full voting rights to vote in all regional and local authority elections. Yes – you read that right, Holyrood in an independent Scotland would continue to be elected by any resident EU member unless the EU agreed to this being changed! The West Lothian Question would become the European Question; any resident EU citizen would have equal rights to determine Scots' future as Scots!

Scottish citizenship would not exist; voting rights would be essentially a residency test for any Commonwealth or EU citizen. This is because the SNP is a socialist party that sees everything through the eyes of the state. Scots alone would not be able to vote on any issue – including leaving the EU – and this creates in my opinion a one way trap door on popular sovereignty. Westminster is Scotland's only constitutional guardian of its right to self determination should it wish for now to remain in the EU, ironic as many Nationalists will find this.

That only people inside Scotland can vote means this a regional rather than national referendum. David Cameron and Alex Salmond have conspired to define what a Scot is and they reject all sense of history or culture in favour of *residency* and that means, of course, that uncontrolled immigration means more "Scots". Alex Salmond is on record to referring to migrants as Scots once they enter Scotland. The UK allows citizens overseas to vote – including those in the armed forces – yet this referendum specifically excludes them.

A Scot post-separation will be anyone who can potentially vote for the SNP. It is that simple.

It is reasonable to infer the SNP has every intention of disenfranchising Scots outside Scotland and if Scotland leaves the EU and remains so then these Scots will lose citizenship overnight. How can one be a free citizen and not be able to vote? It beggars belief that South Sudan's independence vote in 2011 had citizens voting in London – yet Scot's living there will not have a vote this year.

Scotland outside the EU

Outside the EU, Scotland's situation is more complex. By leaving the UK Scotland leaves many other agreements automatically including the EEA, World Trade Organisation and United Nations. It is highly unlikely Scotland would not be allowed to remain a member of the UN and WTO as a sovereign nation by supposition alone. There are no real democratic criteria to entry to the UN and economically speaking Scotland is without question an open and developed trading nation by virtue of UK membership, so entry to the WTO would be a formality.

The EEA is NOT a part of the EU but was signed up to by the UK as an independent nation prior to the Maastricht Treaty, though only by several months. It can be argued that if the EU vetoed Scotland rejoining the EEA or linked it to EU membership it would cause serious ruptions with Switzerland, Iceland and Norway but the legal situation on the EEA is extremely vague. One cannot rule out some hurdles to be overcome but these organisations pool responsibility for issues outwith the member state. They may not interfere in the internal workings of the member state and therefore do not formally encroach on sovereignty in the main.

I openly challenge the Scottish Government to reveal if it has specific advice on EEA membership, independent of membership of the EU.

For the free movement of goods, outside the single market regulations, and free movement of Scots inside the EEA, this MUST be answered. Be aware that the Isle of Man has its own immigration controls and Manx citizens do NOT enjoy freedom of movement of people within the EEA. The Scottish Government must clarify that if it continues EEA membership in supposition that it will be bound fully by its terms and that if it leaves Scots will NOT enjoy freedom of movement within the EEA.

Approaches to Scottish citizenship
Scotland has no right to deprive any Scot of UK citizenship and there is clear precedent here with Irish citizens born before 1922. For as long as Scots remain UK citizens they will enjoy equal treatment within the rest of the UK, though any rights in Scotland will be down to Scottish residency.

Given that a Yes vote for separation would be by a very tight margin and given almost all Scots would retain UK citizenship any attempt by the Scottish Government to further discriminate against UK citizens will create a huge diplomatic headache for it and would not be in its interests. This does not mean it will not do so, simply that it would be irrational and self defeating to do so. The subtle encouragement of anti British feeling will likely continue. Should there be a national movement to redefine Scots in cultural terms, following any rejection of Scottish residency as a suitable form of identity, there is a risk this will generate political conditions as seen in the Republic of Ireland during the last century.

The evidence of Alex Salmond supporting a social union with the UK is lacking. His deputy Nicola Sturgeon has admitted she intends to charge Welsh, Northern Irish and English students tuition fees even *after* separation yet keep them free for other EU citizens. This is not only illegal but specifically *anti-British*. The SNP went further recently and said its childcare policy could not be implemented within the UK because some of the economic gains would go to Westminster. These are the same mimophants that bemoan the Barnet formula at every opportunity so it's clear the social union is already dead in the eyes of the SNP.

Scotland's constitutional relationships with the rest of the UK, EU and EEA have not been defined or explained. The SNP obsesses about maintaining mystery over these matters and its legal advice on the EU. By placing a premium on the information Scots do NOT have, and by suppressing legal advice it leads me to believe the SNP will continue to be unilateral and unprincipled in how it defines the relationship of the Scottish people to the parliament – whereas every unionist party must embrace this chance to renew Holyrood as a servant of the Scottish people.

The SNP will act solely in its own electoral interest: it has every intention of exiling non-resident Scots from future Scottish elections, but inside the EU anyone from Romania or Bulgaria will enjoy full voting rights.

Its *Pulp Fiction* fantasy, Scotland's Future, tells us the SNP cannot distinguish between itself as a party and from Scotland as a whole – and at the same time shows it admits to not believing in true independence at all. The SNP has treated the whole exercise as a show of self importance and it must be seen now to hold the social union of the UK in contempt.

All unionists must demand access to our common legal advice on the EU, that the Scottish Government commissions advice on the EEA at once and explains why the Scottish Government's view of people outside its borders is less than that of Sudan's.

The SNP's policies on children, young families and students are especially callous and egregious given how vulnerable these groups are. They have sought to use and encourage the vulnerability of the poorest Scots to spite politicians in Westminster; not able to turn water to wine the SNP turn suffering into havering and blethering. Scots should be in no doubt how the Nationalists intend to punish the vulnerable for daring to vote No. They cannot offer real citizenship if they win the referendum and *face having no childcare policy when they lose.*

My call to residents of Scotland who are undecided about how they will vote in the upcoming referendum is to hear the call of Scots denied that vote outside our nation by the SNP and lend them theirs. (The same Scots that are granted a vote in Westminster elections by the UK government.) They should contact any Scot that they know living abroad or in rest of the UK and vote on their behalf. It is better all our votes are used and counted so that this referendum be as decisive as it truly needs to be.

From the Dean's Diaries: The Dean and the United Kingdom

Professor D.W. Purdie
14 January 2014

Office of the Dean:

St Andrew's College,
King George IV Bridge,
Edinburgh EH1 3TD

IT HAD to happen sooner or later. Desperate for celebrity endorsement - even from the grave - our National Bard has been resurrected, reanimated and re-programmed to trumpet and champion Independence. In Saturday's *Herald* there appeared an article on Prof Robert Crawford of St Andrews University who has apparently written a book entitled *Bannockburns*.

Apart from the dreadful title, degrading not one but two of our revered institutions, the piece insinuated that Burns was effectively, a liar. His letters, verse and songs which supported the Revolution Settlement of 1688 and the constitution as settled by the Union, are false. They are the pathetic whinings of a placeman, a civil servant crouching in the train of authority, and desperate to keep his job as an officer of the Excise. All the time, apparently, he was actually in *favour* of a breakup of the Union he claimed to defend with a view to establishing an independent Scotland.

Burns thus was a cynical hypocrite, prepared to sink to rank mendacity to keep his nose clean. Worse, he must have perjured himself in his Oath of Allegiance to the Crown when he joined the Royal Dumfries Volunteers, falsely promising to defend a United Kingdom he actually wished to see dismembered.

Burns was no hypocrite ; he was an honest man and prized honesty and plain dealing above all other virtues – as shines out from the verses of, *A Man's a Man for a' that'* his great Anthem for the Common Man -.

"He showed my youth," wrote William Wordsworth, a firm admirer, "how verse could build a princely throne – on humble Truth!"

Prof Crawford, says *The Herald* is to be commended for 'picking through the poems with a fine tooth comb' to discover 'prime examples of Burns showing his patriotic tendencies.' These prime examples discovered by Crawford's fine comb include *Scots Wha Hae!* This song, whose correct title is *Robert Brice's March to Bannockburn*, does not display 'tendency' – it is a magnificent shout of defiance at an alien invader, our ancestors well aware that what awaited them on that field was either a gory bed – or victory.

"You will gain that field," the Bruce told them, "or you will lie beneath it for ever. Forward."

Constitutional freedom came with the Treaty of Northampton in 1328 which ended the War and recognised Scotland a sovereign independent State. Of course Burns took the Scottish part in what had been a military campaign; of course he advocated armed resistance to invasion, occupation and subjection. But what on earth has that to do with our present constitutional debate?

Another song cited by Crawford being in favour of sundering

the Union is; *A Parcel of Rogues in a Nation*. Burns was certainly highly critical of some of the tactics used to secure the votes necessary to send the Scots Parliament into its 300 year recess – and so am I. What happened was often disgraceful, but the *outcome* is what matters. Did we descend again into invasion, occupation and subjection? No we did not.

The Union, as Burns well knew, gave us two tremendous assets: it gave us peace; peace after five centuries of cross-border warfare, untold misery and loss of life and property. But above all, it gave us the markets. Markets for our greatest asset; the intelligence, energy, inventiveness and endurance of our people. They first moved south to positions of power in England and then swept out to all corners of the Empire as adventurers, soldiers, governors and merchants.

Some rogues there were indeed at the foundation, but their roguery was to produce results for the new Union which neither nation could have produced alone.

Let me conclude with the last days of the Bard. He died of untreated rheumatic heart disease and terminal endocarditis in Dumfries. It was the summer of 1796 and he was 37 years old.

He was buried in St Michael's kirkyard in Dumfries with full military honours, as befitted a serving soldier in a Territorial Army unit, The Royal Dumfries Volunteers. He and his comrades were prepared to fight for, and if necessary to die in defence of, the United Kingdom, the Union.

For it was neither England nor Scotland that saw off Napoleon Bonaparte in Burns's day; it was the Union. It was neither England nor Scotland in 1940 that spat defiance in the faces of Hitler and his gang; it was the Union. And it was the Union, with its allies, led by the United States, that faced down the Warsaw Pact.

And, finally, in our own day. Is England, or Scotland, a Permanent Member of the Security Council of the United Nations..? No, it is neither. It is that oldest, most enduring and most successful Union of two distinct Nations in world history.

Burns was a Union man; and if there was any doubt it lies in the smash-hit Song of the year 1795 which was sung all over a Union then threatened with invasion from across the Channel. Guess who wrote it:

Does haughty Gaul Invasion threat?
    Then let the loons *beware*, sir!
There's wooden Walls upon our Seas,
    And Volunteers on Shore, sir!

Be Britain still to Britain true,
    Amang ourselves *united* !
But never but by *British* hands,
    Maun British wrangs be righted….

Amen to that.

Danny Alexander and the two missing words

Bill Jamieson
14 January 2014

SO THAT'S SETTLED: a worry for the markets has been removed. The UK will continue to honour Scotland's debts "in all circumstances" *(sic)* even if it votes for independence. No need, then, for investors to fret and attach a risk premium to UK debt.

Alex Salmond is cock-a-hoop. He feels the UK government's bluff has been pulled. Scotland's contribution to UK debt interest charges and repayments will be settled by negotiation. The consensus view is that the Treasury has lost a negotiating hand. The chancellor has warned that currency sharing may not be at all practicable. But how can he now credibly oppose the SNP's proposal to continue to share the UK currency after independence if he wants Scotland to contribute to the debt servicing bill?

In truth, very little has been settled on an issue that has the capacity to destabilise the public finances and poison relations between Scotland the rest of the UK for a generation.

It is the division of this colossal debt on independence – standing currently at £1.38 trillion and set to rise on OBR calculations to £1.58 trillion (86 per cent of UK GDP) by 2016-17, the year of possible independence – that will test the Holyrood and Westminster administrations to the limit.

What exactly has been "settled" that could defuse this ticking bomb? The method by which UK public debt is measured – what it includes and what it doesn't – has still to be determined. So, too, is agreement on how Scotland's share of that debt is to be calculated (population or historic spending share) and the precise calculation of what is "fair and proportionate".

As for UK assets, how are these to be divided and what might they include? North Sea oil revenues would almost certainly form the basis of a powerful Scottish claim. But what of the financial assets to which Alex Salmond referred this week – the UK's gold and foreign reserves? The Treasury's contingency reserve? What of defence and security assets? And all the physical assets such as land and buildings currently held by the UK government and hundreds of UK public bodies and government outcrops, both here in Scotland and overseas?

Of course Alex Salmond will be keen to ensure that Scotland negotiates an advantageous deal – the lowest possible share of UK public debt and the highest possible share of UK assets. And it would be in no-one's interest to saddle Scotland with debt obligations it would be unable to fulfil.

But as important as Scottish sensitivities are those across the rest of the UK. Voters in England, Wales and Ulster may feel they have no moral or legal duty to cut the Scots a favourable deal or agree to a settlement that prejudices their own interests, particularly if, as a consequence of independence the rUK share of GDP falls and its debt-to-GDP ratio rises further. And it is the concerns of international creditors and this greater number of taxpayers that will be well to the fore among Treasury ministers.

Debt – and debt servicing costs – are concerns over which debate on Scottish public finance has been largely innocent. Little if any mention can be found in the Scottish government budget statements. MSPs barely mention public debt obligations. Spending decisions are uncluttered by such considerations.

Yet debt is the largest and most pressing issue in modern public finance. Whatever agreement is arrived at on how an independent Scotland will service its share, the annual cost of debt interest alone will cast a shadow over all departmental budgets. The Scottish government's White Paper calculates a historical share of debt interest could be £5.5 billion in 2016-17 on a per head share basis – close to the annual total Scotland's spends on education.

Alex Salmond breezily dismisses this debt as a product of the extravagance of Labour and Conservative administrations in London, largesse of which Scotland was entirely innocent. Yet it is this resort to debt finance on a scale without precedent in modern times that has helped to finance Scotland's ever rising Barnet settlements and provided successive Holyrood administrations with the fuel for public spending. Has the SNP ever declined higher public spending from Westminster? Has it not urged more of it at every opportunity?

What of liabilities outwith the debt total? The ONS calculates the UK Public Sector Gross Debt at around £1.4 trillion, not including liabilities due to other types of instruments (e.g., derivatives or accounts payable). It only covers the financial liabilities accrued as a result of past government activity and does not capture expected future liabilities from past government action, such as public sector pension obligations, or nuclear decommissioning costs. These are substantial and would be subject to detailed scrutiny. Nor does it consider contingent liabilities of the UK Government, such as guarantees the UK government provides. There is another issue. All measures of debt in the public accounts are not "marked to market" Yet it is the market value of UK debt that represents the present value of the liability and includes the cost of future interest payments. At current interest rates the market value of most UK debt is greater than the nominal redemption value recorded in the public accounts. That is, they do not reflect the current market value of the debt. Instead, they reflect the nominal value of the debt at maturity.

The Scottish Government's Fiscal Commission Working Group calculated that, on a population basis, Scotland's share of UK public sector net debt in 2017-18 would be worth £126 billion, equivalent to 72 per cent of Scottish GDP. This is slightly lower than the equivalent UK figure of 77 per cent. This would be quite manageable – assuming it secures the lion's share of North Sea oil revenues and that these revenues are sustained well into the future.

The negotiations post independence will thus be critical in determining Scotland's financial fortunes. But they also have the potential to fuel deep resentment either side of the Border. The negotiations would need to assure international creditors that any debt settlement arrived at is solid, durable and robust. Treasury Chief Secretary Danny Alexander said this week that the assurance that UK debt was essential to prevent investors charging a 'separation surcharge' for lending to the UK. But given all the unresolved issues ahead, his statement that the Treasury would guarantee Scotland's share of that £1.4 trillion of debt "in all circumstances" (sic) arguably omitted two critical words: *"for now"*.

A tale of two unions

Stuart Winton
16 January 2014

ONE OF THE more bizarre aspects of the Yes campaign for Scottish independence is its differing approaches to the UK and EU.

Thus a referendum on EU membership is regarded as an awful prospect, and a consequent Britexit simply doesn't bear thinking about. Don't even consider the prospects for trade if we were outside the European single market, while apparently we're all appalled at the thought of losing EU citizenship. How difficult would it be to extricate us from the political, economic and legal ties binding us to Europe? And how could an independent Scotland possibly be 'expelled' from the EU anyway?

On the other hand, a referendum on Scotland's UK membership is regarded as the means to ending centuries of serfdom and subjugation under the heel of perfidious Albion. In an independent Scotland trade with the residual UK would be a breeze, lost UK citizenship and the impact on the social union of little real relevance or concern. By the same token, separating Scotland from the UK would be largely unproblematic, while the language of exclusion and expulsion is replaced by emancipation and freedom.

The reality is that both the UK and EU are political and economic unions to a greater or lesser extent, where members share or pool sovereignty. The institutions and mechanisms governing both are hardly identical, but fundamentally the entities are not dissimilar.

Of course, that's not to say that membership of both is equally desirable, so how might they be compared? As someone who feels under siege from politicians at all levels and of all parties I'm not predisposed to getting all Deerin-esque[1] or dewy-eyed about the UK, but how about a few largely indisputable basic facts? Thus the UK as a political and economic union has lasted 300 years and is relatively stable. Indeed its sterling currency stands eloquent testimony to this.

By contrast, the EU's longevity in its current form can barely be measured in decades, never mind centuries. It has already faced a huge existential crisis, largely the result of its ill-thought out currency union, which has had catastrophic implications for the economies of several member states.

Unsurprisingly, then, despite the Yes campaign's juxtaposition of the unmitigated bad of the UK with the unalloyed good of the EU, Scottish public opinion would seem to favour the former over the latter. Based, presumably, on an objective and rational analysis rather than on closed minds and crude emotion.

The currency issue neatly demonstrates the SNP's inconsistency and hypocrisy on matters of sovereignty. It is not that long since Alex Salmond was describing sterling as a 'millstone' round Scotland's neck, and that Bank of England interest rates were geared towards the economy of London and the south-east of England. But, and consistent with the foregoing, the SNP's answer to this was eurozone membership for Scotland, with interest rates set by the European Central Bank in Frankfurt.

Of course, you don't need to be an expert on monetary policy to see the inherent contradiction there, and indeed since the eurozone nearly collapsed Mr Salmond has neatly volte-faced and now sterling is claimed to be one of Scotland's assets rather than a liability. Mr Salmond quotes Keynes' dictum that "when the facts change, I change my mind". But surely a more objective and compelling characterisation is that the facts proved Mr Salmond misjudged the whole euro project. Indeed, the eurozone problems to an extent actually proved the first minister's point regarding his original complaint about the inappropriateness of Bank of England monetary policy for Scotland, albeit on a larger and more catastrophic scale.

Mr Salmond has, however, latterly changed his rhetoric to perhaps more realistically reflect the more nuanced environment of sovereignty pooled in supra-national entities such as the UK, EU and Nato. Thus he has said that Scotland would remain part of five unions, which better reflects the reality of the SNP's aim rather than the former faintly ludicrous notion of 'independence in Europe', albeit that in the event of a Yes vote the idea that Scotland would be genuinely independent is increasingly fanciful.

But even accepting all this begs several questions relating to what was mentioned at the outset, most obviously the unquestioning attitude towards the EU as compared to the relentless negativity as regards the UK. After all, even ignoring the currency issue, last year the European Parliament bragged that, "with the majority of laws being shaped at EU level, the Parliament is now at least as powerful as any national parliament".

Thus it's perhaps instructive that while Yes campaigners persistently question the future direction of the UK, the EU's extensive sovereignty over national legislatures is simply ignored. A related point – and perhaps just as important as the debate over an independent Scotland's terms of EU membership, which the SNP prefers to brush over – is whether the EU is moving further towards a United States of Europe or in fact heading in the opposite direction of repatriating sovereignty to member states. Of course, there is some discussion of such matters in the context of the UK's EU membership, but don't bother looking for it in relation to Scotland's 'independence'.

And while the future direction of Europe is one thing, the Yes double standard is also evident with regard to other aspects of EU unmentionables. Thus the UK is deemed undemocratic, while the largely unelected and more unaccountable EU institutions are fine and dandy. The UK is unequal and its parliament remote it is claimed, while Scotland would have a place at the top table in Europe, despite the reality that it would be near-invisible in the EU's unelected institutions, not to mention what would amount to marginal representation in the European Parliament. By the same token, the UK's Supreme Court is seen as out of touch and unrepresentative, while the European Court of Justice is simply never considered worth mentioning.

But it goes without saying that many Yes campaigners will characterise the analysis above as Europhobic or even xenophobic. Of course, by their standards the Yes campaign could equally be described in such terms, albeit substituting *Anglophobia* for Europhobia.

Likewise, in the rare event of Yes campaigners actually addressing UK/EU comparisons, attempts are usually made to distinguish the two, but the arguments adduced usually tend towards the theoretical, hair-splitting and contrived. In the final analysis, it's all about where best to share sovereignty and ensuring democratic consent thereto. For example, the absolute sovereignty of the UK's parliament is often compared to the supposedly more consensual nature of the EU, but again the irony here is that the same people welcome a referendum on Scotland in the UK, but react with horror to the prospect of the public being asked to democratically decide the UK's future in the EU.

But the debate should be about where sovereignty is best pooled, and not simply assumed that sharing power in Brussels is inherently a good thing, while doing likewise in London is necessarily bad. Of course, the SNP does now want certain powers to reside at the UK level, but in the context of its stance more generally, and as demonstrated by the currency issue in particular, the party often looks opportunist and inconsistent.

To sum up, like perhaps most people, I see pros and cons in both the EU and UK, but Yes campaigners tend to view these entities exclusively in terms of pros and cons respectively. As regards encouraging an open and honest debate on Scotland's future, I personally think that's a bit of a con.

[1] http://www.theguardian.com/commentisfree/2014/jan/13/scots-moral-duty-stay-british-referendum

Will it all be over in September?

Murdo Fraser
18 January 2014

MY LABOUR CHUM Ian Smart wrote an entertaining blog this week[1] offering some (rather tongue in cheek) advice for Eddie Barnes, the new Head of Strategy and Communications for the Scottish Conservatives. I don't intend to comment in any detail on most of Ian's recommendations (the last thing that the Party needs is a running commentary from me), but there was one line in it that did cause me to reflect.

Ian states "Forget the constitution. That will be settled on 18th September". Will it? Certainly there are many people on the Unionist side of the debate who would share Ian's hope that 18th September will mark the end of the constitutional debate in Scotland.

It has been a source of frustration for years now for those of us in Scottish politics, but not in the SNP, that the constitutional debate has completely dominated public discourse, squeezing out important conversations on a whole range of other issues: creating a more enterprising economy, tackling poverty, improving the public services, creating a world class infrastructure. It would be great to think that after 18th September we could get back to focussing on these vital issues.

So let us look at the various scenarios, starting with the extremely unlikely, and very unwelcome, prospect of a Yes vote.

I don't accept that even if there is a Yes vote in the referendum that this will mean the end of the constitutional debate. All a Yes vote will do is signal the start of what will be very protracted negotiations with the rest of the UK over currency, national debt, cross-border trade, and a whole host of other vital matters. At the same time, there will have to be negotiations with the EU over the terms of Scottish membership, and negotiations with other international organisations such as the UN and NATO. Far from a Yes vote being the end of constitutional discussions, it will just open the door to these being even more dominant than they have been over the past years.

Let us turn to the more likely scenario of a No vote. I suspect, given where we are now, if the Yes campaign were to achieve 40 per cent in the final vote they would regard that as a pretty good outcome. 40 per cent or more of the public voting Yes would be taken by them as a launch pad for the next referendum, however many years distant that might be. Nicola Sturgeon has already hinted that this is on the SNP agenda, and indeed it would be incredible if it that were not to be the case.

We would most likely find ourselves in a situation like Quebec, where for the next 15 or more years our political debate would be dominated by the constitutional question, with the SNP looking for an opportunity, were they again to form a government at Holyrood, to hold a second referendum when they deemed the time to be right. This would be a dismal prospect for all. So, a No vote in the referendum but with a chunky percentage for Yes will certainly mean that the debate is not over.

That leaves us with a third option, a comprehensive win for No with the Yes vote below 40 per cent. In that scenario, talk of another referendum would look ridiculous. But I do not think that even this means the end of the constitutional debate.

The Scotland Act will already devolve substantial additional financial powers to Holyrood from 2015. In addition to this, all three Unionist parties are currently looking at proposals for what further devolution might be delivered in the event of a No vote. The Liberal Democrats have already proposed their own version of Home Rule. Both Labour and Conservatives have commissions working on this due to report in the Spring. So even a substantial No victory in the referendum will mean further powers being devolved.

And that will not mark the end of the road. Because what I suspect will happen is that devolution of further power to Scotland will be a catalyst for a broader constitutional discussion across the United Kingdom. Already we are seeing people in Wales asking why they cannot have the same devolved powers as in Scotland. We have seen Boris Johnson, Mayor of London, arguing for devolution of certain legislative powers to the capital.

The Scottish Conservative leader, Ruth Davidson, has suggested that there should be a UK-wide commission to look at the constitution after a No vote. This seems to me a very sensible way to proceed.

Incidentally, it has always been my view that the offer of further devolution in the event of a no vote will have an influence on the outcome of the referendum. A YouGov poll commissioned by Better Together, and published last week, showed that 30 per cent of Scots backed independence, while 29 per cent supported the status quo, and 32 per cent wanted stronger devolution. A credible proposal of further devolution in the event of a No vote will ensure that these 32 per cent are firmly voting No, thus ensuring overwhelming victory, and killing off for good the prospect of separation.

It is quite clear from this poll and similar surveys that have been done that the "centre of gravity" of Scottish public opinion is for devolution, with greater powers. Some of those currently tempted to vote "Yes" would settle for this as an option, while those who prefer the status quo would regard it as preferable to independence. This is the common ground on which we should be advancing.

So what I think is clear is that on September the 18th we will settle the vital question as to whether Scotland remains part of the United Kingdom, or not. But it will not mark the end of the debate on the constitution. I know that will disappoint Ian, and probably many others, but I am afraid that that is the reality.

[1] http://ianssmart.blogspot.co.uk/2014/01/advice-for-eddie.html

No vote and no choice offered on Scottish citizenship

Liz Smith
21 January 2014

IN RECENT WEEKS, the Referendum debate has, not surprisingly, mainly revolved around the issues which relate to the economy, the EU and defence. To give credit to both the Yes and No camps, the start of 2014 seems to have sharpened the focus for debate; in the case of the Yes camp, there has been a recognition that the Scottish public is wanting much more detail in response to what independence would really mean, and, in the case of the No camp, there has been a recognition that the public expects to hear more about the positive reasons for staying within the UK rather than just about the dangers of independence.

It is also clear – again probably not surprisingly – that many more people outwith the political villages of Holyrood and Westminster are beginning to make their voices heard; whether they come from the business community, academic institutions, the arts world, sport, entertainment or the voluntary sector. That too, is a good thing since it allows voters to hear a fresh perspective, a bit removed from the relentless, partisan daily exchanges from politicians.

But a third thing has happened in recent weeks and that is the growing interest and participation in the debate about independence from non-Scottish British citizens and also from Scots living outwith Scotland. Those who were born in other parts of the UK and who now reside in Scotland, and those Scots who live in the rest of the UK and abroad want to know what their position would be if there was a Yes vote.

On pages 271-273 of the White Paper "Scotland's Future" it says that "deciding who is a citizen is a defining characteristic of an independent state." It also says that within an independent Scotland there would be "an inclusive model of citizenship" so that all those who wished to retain other national identities could do so. In the UK just now you can hold dual (or multiple citizenship) so, on that level, it seems perfectly in order for an independent Scotland to do the same.

But read on in the section and we find that what is actually planned is that all British citizens permanently resident in Scotland would have to become Scottish citizens as well, whether they liked it or not. Scottish born British citizens currently living outside Scotland would also be considered Scottish citizens, again, whether they liked it or not.

In other words, an Englishman, permanently resident in Scotland has to become a Scottish citizen even if he has no wish to be anything other than British. So too will a Scottish born person, permanently resident in another part of the UK or abroad.

These people would like an answer, not least because the section which deals with this in the White Paper is entitled "the choices open to us". Do they have a choice or is the SNP really saying that it will force those born in Scotland but living in the rest of the UK or abroad to become Scottish citizens even though they have no vote in the referendum?

This seems very undemocratic to many people and they want to know why they cannot have any say in the matter. Some are even questioning whether the SNP's plans would be consistent with EU law. They are saying that, in the event of independence, those who want to be Scottish but who live outwith Scotland should be able to apply for Scottish citizenship, but it should not be forced upon them.

For months now, the Scottish Government has been discriminating against rest of the UK students. Despite repeated questioning at Holyrood by a dozen or so MSPs from all opposition parties, they have singularly failed to explain how they will be allowed to maintain this policy in an independent Scotland given that EU law says that it would be illegal for a Scottish Government to discriminate between rest of the UK students and those who come from the EU.

It is generally accepted that governments – of whatever political hue – are not obliged to publish their legal advice, so the SNP is quite within its rights not to do so. The only trouble is that on many of the really big questions about what independence might mean, voter sight of that key evidence would make a huge difference to the information process and whether they decide to vote yes or no.

The more the SNP goes on telling us that everything it says in the White Paper is consistent with EU law yet it is unwilling to prove it, the more dangerous a tightrope its politicians are walking.

Indyref: Hold, sell or buy?

Bill Jamieson
22 January 2014

AMONG THE myriad of questions posed by the independence referendum is the reaction of financial markets. Would a 'Yes' vote trigger a sell-off in gilts and equities? Would the UK currency take a hit?

For now the continuing dominance of the 'No' vote in opinion polls has kept the implications of a break-up of the UK well below the radar of investor concerns. The main preoccupations continue to centre on interest rates, China (of course) and whether recent company profit warnings might trigger a sell-off on the stock market.

An assessment this week by Walbrook Economics, a London-based independent economic consultancy, is one of the first to consider the implications for investors. Written by analyst Ewen Stewart, it concludes that a break-up of the UK would be "modestly bad news" for sterling and UK gilts in the short term "with a sub five per cent sell off likely".

Much of the analysis will be familiar to Scottish readers. The finances of an independent Scotland critically depend on the outcome of negotiations on the share of oil revenues, the division of the UK's £1.2 trillion debt and agreement on currency sharing.

The loss to the remainder of the UK of £127 billion of GDP (8.4 per cent of the total) would relegate it to sixth place in the global league, behind France. Oil revenues would be proportionately far more important to an independent Scotland. But with swings in the oil price, they have varied between four and 22 per cent of Scottish tax revenues – a huge swing factor for any future Scottish chancellor. As for debt share, a calculation based on population share would leave Scotland with £100 billion or 8.4 per cent of the current UK total. As a proportion of Scottish GDP, this, at 79 per cent would be manageable, but the cost of debt servicing and big cyclical swings in oil revenues would pose problems for a future government's spending ambitions.

As for the impact on rUK, break-up would be seen as "a profound event, given the UK's perceived safe haven status, and although it would be of secondary importance as to whether to invest in the UK in general, or London in particular... would be a marginal negative to overall perceptions."

However, looking at the political consequences, while the final outcome of a 'Yes' vote may well be "a sub five per cent sell-off" , it is extremely difficult for analysts to predict the market volatility that may result from a 'Yes' vote. While there would be no constitutional requirement for the coalition government to fall, Stewart's view is that David Cameron "would have no option but to resign". That would give bond market investors much to think about. The referendum terms, he writes, "were decided on his watch, and for the nation to suffer such a seismic shift without 'falling on his sword' would be unthinkable in terms of real politik."

Meanwhile, somewhere in the middle of this maelstrom the rUK government needs to agree a cross-party negotiating team to resolve the huge questions of oil revenue division, debt apportionment, currency sharing, division of defence assets and future pension welfare and pension obligations. The SNP belief that these negotiations could be concluded in 18 months to declare dissolution of the Union on March 24 2016 is, says Stewart, "very ambitious". That's putting it mildly.

As for the impact on UK equities, "we believe it would only have a modest, short-term impact on equity markets generally" – less than five per cent of FTSE revenues, in aggregate, originate from Scotland. The energy sector is reckoned to face the greatest 'independence risk' while financial service companies with significant operations and cost bases in Scotland "would be heavily challenged under independence".

The implications for us living and working in Scotland are, of course, far, far more alarming. The financial sector in Scotland generates around £8 billion for the Scottish economy and employs almost 100,000 people directly and around the same again indirectly. It manages more than £800 billion of funds with major companies such as Standard Life, Scottish Widows, Alliance, Baillie Gifford, Martin Currie and others.

With around 90 per cent of Scottish financial sector business generated outside of Scotland, institutional and private clients alike will need every assurance on how regulation might work. Will there be extra costs for the industry with Scotland setting up its own regulator, and to which regulatory authority would firms be answerable? Concern over both tax and currency risk could not only act as a deterrent for rUK clients but could also see a withdrawal of funds. Unless full safeguards and guarantees are given, Scotland could see one of its key sectors melt away before its eyes. In that event, a "sub five per cent" gilt sell-off would be the least of our worries.

What price Mr Swinney's economic levers?

Eben Wilson
24 January 2014

A CLEVER piece of work has just been released by two economists from Stirling University. It looks at an issue central to the referendum debate – the "fairness and equality" agenda. They examined "The extent to which the government of a small open country or semi-autonomous region can achieve a different level of income inequality from the wider equality of which it is part".

That is, can Scotland's government or devolved administration use re-distributive or fiscal policy to generate "fairness and equality"?

Such policies are often voiced in Scotland as part of a perceived cultural tradition; a democratic desire to have a "Common Weal" as the Reid Foundation put it, to rid us of inequalities that are unjust. Our centre-left commentariat also point to a Nordic model of redistribution and equality as a policy goal.

Analysing equality is a viciously complicated area of study, but the Stirling work is painstaking. They make a number of interesting points.

With respect to the extent of income redistribution, the UK is actually above the OECD average, but we start with a slightly more unequal initial position. We would therefore need more "equalising" through redistribution to get to a Nordic position.

Gross and net income inequality in the OECD [figure]

OECD income inequality (GINI coefficient) is shown as the full bar, with the red bar as the re-distributed portion of all incomes.

The study looked at a range of earners, seeking measures of behavioural responses – specifically what change in work patterns and what migration might result from tax rises. The expected responses were varied across income levels based on other key empirical evidence.

The results make fascinating reading, showing that the use of economic levers is not quite as powerful as many might expect with respect to adjusting measures of equality.

Adding a penny to the higher rate of tax raises virtually no revenue.

Adding a penny to the standard rate produces a small amount of revenue, but across such a large cohort of taxpayers.

Reducing the threshold of a higher 50 per cent rate of tax from £150,000 to £100,000 actually *reduces* total revenues.

In each case, the change in inequality measures is minimal.

So, it seems that "making the pips squeak" among higher earners would be rather unproductive in Scotland. Migration and work substitution effects alone, the study says, reduce potential revenue by fully 75 per cent. The pips flee, they don't squeak.

In fact, in my view, the study underestimates a large further impact on economic efficiency on the supply-side. The model used leaves out decisions about whether to work or not as a result of a tax change, nor the reaction of firms to tax changes. Neither do they incorporate a calculation specifically related to the self-employed of whom there are twice as many in Scotland as in

Nordic countries and in my view are particularly elastic in their response to tax changes.

Nor do they evaluate additional dynamic supply-side effects of the loss of high-earners through migration. There is a concept in dynamic system analysis of "network effects". In industry and commerce these would be heavily weighted to knowledge within local supply chains; where knowledge includes not only how to do something, but who to do it with, and how to do it profitably. For Scotland, losing top earners through migration would be disastrous for strategic supply chain development, losing middle earners would be disastrous for technical supply chain retention, and losing work effort would be disastrous for productivity generally.

Sadly, the dream of a Nordic paradise with a high level of equality (which many will tell you actually does not actually exist in Scandinavia, the top 1 per cent in Sweden for example earn 9 per cent of income, just a little below that of the UK) appears not to be available through a mechanistic fiscal lever-pulling exercise. The difficulty for Scotland is that a strong political tendency has adopted "fairness and equality" as a policy goal, based on fathomless reasoning. The Common Weal project offers this analysis:

"Because so much is taken by so few at the very top of society, a majority of the population is less wealthy than it should be."[1]

This fallacy that the poor are poor because the rich are rich is a widespread and nonsensical myth that goes back to the time of the Enclosure Acts and Luddites. Were it true, the few would have become fewer through time, while the majority would have become almost everyone – this process of the "immiseration of the masses" actually fell apart around 1851 when Karl Marx falsified the evidence he used in Das Capital from the Poor Law audits he was studying. The figures in that year began to show that scarcer labour was being paid more; Marx chose to ignore that, in essence ignoring the role of human and physical capital in generating revenue.

The Common Weal group do actually recognise the limitations of fiscal redistributions, but they too have a false view of capital.

"The best way to redistribute wealth is not to take cash from one person and give it to another, but to raise tax progressively and use it to create good jobs in the public sector. These good jobs underpin much of the rest of the domestic economy, so in fact the public sector is one of the most important wealth-creating sectors we have. The more jobs we create in the public sector, the more wealth is redistributed and the more the overall economy is stimulated."

The fallacy here is in the term "good jobs". It's a subjective remark, essentially meaning work at wage levels that are not inadequate. But that does not mean that they are wealth-creating; yes, a borough engineer who puts in a set of traffic lights may make local transport more efficient for business, but that's a long way from saying that the return to those traffic improvements is greater than the losses created elsewhere by higher progressive taxes. The issue comes down to the choices made between public sector activity and private sector activity and the return to capital employed in each case. That's where the earnings are generated, and the distribution of those earnings is related to value-adding productivity and the scarcity of labour. The public sector is in fact famous for producing a large quantity of low paid jobs; pay is perennially rationed across public services because of inefficiency in the way capital is employed.

The neo-Keynesian notion in their last sentence that an economy is stimulated by redistributing wealth to the public sector appears to be being disproven (yet again) at the moment as spending constraint is replaced by private sector economic growth. This is probably due to the fact that many choices of activity by the public sector are both revenue consuming and unproductive because they are not priced for consumers to approve them as choices.

So, if we cannot reduce inequality by taxing people, nor by moving activity into the public sector, how can we improve equality measures? Again, the answer has to be through better capital and better use of capital. Today, that means harnessing knowledge and skills and making investment risks less risky. The state has notably failed in both its ability to educate the populace relevantly for productive work and in its own attempts, such as intermediate technology institutes, to subsidise investment risk. It also taxes both labour and capital productivity massively through National Insurance and corporate taxes respectively. Political lever pulling is hugely wasteful, inefficient and beset by vested interests determined to line their own income nests.

The answer then is for the state to cut taxes and get out of the way. In Scotland, we need to let capital work much much harder on behalf of choices made by risk-takers. Spending money investing in people and things privately across the board and then re-investing it again and again is the way to make all corks rise.

As for fairness and equality, it's a strange measure. I know people who value leisure highly who will only work so many hours in a week; I know others who love the productive chase so much that they never stop. They have a mix of productive talents and some of those who work less are worth more than those who work hard. I expect they all value each other equally as human beings. My focus on fairness and equality would be to free those stuck at the bottom of the income scale through state incompetence by allowing the better off the freedom to explore productive tomorrows. A good technician in a technical world is worth his or her weight in gold and I respect them enormously. We all need each other, and we particularly need new improving and learning staff. Raising demand for them across the board is the way to decrease inequalities.

---

[1] http://www.allofusfirst.org/the-key-ideas/creating-a-more-equal-society/

Carney demolishes SNP currency argument

Murdo Fraser
29 January 2014

IT HAS ALWAYS seemed to me self-evident that one of the features of a nation state is that it should have its own currency. The reason why many UK Conservatives opposed British membership of the Euro in the 1990s was for precisely this reason: it would involve a substantial ceding of national sovereignty, including vital economic levers such as the ability to set interest rates in accordance with the needs of the national economy. That scepticism towards the Euro is now widely shared across the political spectrum, encompassing even previously Euro-enthusiast parties such as the Liberal Democrats and the SNP.

So the logic of the argument for an independent Scotland must surely be for that independent country to have its own currency. This is a position adopted by many elements in the Yes Campaign, including the Green Party, the Socialists, and the Yes Scotland Chairman Dennis Canavan. It is undoubtedly the logical view to hold for those advocating independence, particularly those who have spent their political careers railing against the whole concept of Scotland being tied to the pound sterling, and having interest rates set by the Bank of England in London tailored to the needs of the whole UK economy rather than specifically to the needs of Scotland.

But this is not, of course, the SNP position. Its once favoured policy of joining the Euro is no longer credible, not least as it is hugely unpopular with the public. In any event, joining the Euro would require an independent Scotland not just to meet the stringent convergent criteria, but also to have its own separate currency for at least three years. So that is not an option at present.

Having a separate Scottish currency, however logical a step that might be, has been ruled out by the SNP worried about the response from Scottish businesses to the prospect of their major export market (the rest of the UK) operating in a different currency zone, with all the implications that has for additional costs, risks of currency fluctuation etc. Moreover, having a separate currency does not fit with the SNP separatist agenda which is about "de-risking" independence by trying to portray it as a minor change with as few significant consequences as possible. Having the pound still in our pocket would, they think, make independence more palatable.

That leaves the SNP with the policy of a monetary union with the rest of the UK, with the Bank of England issuing our currency, setting our interest rates, and being the lender of last resort. Such an arrangement is theoretically possible, but carries with it all sorts of risks both for Scotland and the rest of the UK ("rUK") should it happen. And it is difficult to find any historical precedent for a successful monetary union where there are two partners, one of whom has an economy effectively ten times the size of the other.

One of the first questions that has to be answered is: why would the rest of the UK want to enter a monetary union with Scotland on this basis? With the relative size of each economy, rUK could bail out Scotland in the event of an economic crisis, but not vice versa. It is self-evident that this creates a moral hazard.

Why would the Government of rUK wish to expose itself (and its people) to such a risk? Even if it were prepared to consider the possibility, rUK would have to put very stringent conditions on Scotland in the event of monetary union, particularly around budget issues such as borrowing and spending limits, to protect its own people and economy.

As for the Scottish perspective, whilst a monetary union would in theory involve shared decision making with the Bank of England, if rUK had 90 per cent of the votes and Scotland 10 per cent, Scotland's influence would close to zero when it came to any vital and contentious matters. Moreover, the costs of borrowing in Scotland would be bound to be higher than in rUK, as Scotland (as the smaller partner) would be deemed by the markets as more likely to default (remember the White Paper makes it explicit – see p.111 – that Scotland could choose to unilaterally dissolve the monetary union *at any time*).

In a speech in Edinburgh today, the Governor of the Bank of England, Mark Carney, reinforced some of these concerns. He drew attention to the moral hazard problem saying that this "suggests the need for tight fiscal rules, to enforce the prudent behaviour for all in the union, although credible sanctions for breaking those rules are hard to develop". He went on to say, "the degree of fiscal risk sharing will likely have to be significant".

Carney drew a parallel with the situation in the Eurozone where the evidence has been that a monetary union requires a high degree of political integration underpinning it in order to be successful. He said "it is no coincidence that effective currency unions tend to have centralised fiscal authorities whose spending is a sizeable share of GDP", concluding "in short, a durable, successful currency union requires some ceding of national sovereignty".

In many respects, this was stating the obvious. But it is important to have the message reinforced, and to have it done so from such a substantial figure as the Governor of the Bank of England gives it additional credibility.

It is without doubt from the academic research which has been done, and confirmed by Mark Carney today, that the monetary union envisaged by the SNP would, even if possible, only work with a substantial restriction on the freedom of operation of the government of an independent Scotland. It is highly questionable whether, for example, the rUK Government would agree to an independent Scotland cutting Corporation Tax rates below the rUK level.

Independence, if it means anything, must surely mean having control over one's country's economic levers. That is what the SNP have told us for years. But it is now clear that monetary union with the rest of the UK in no way represents independence as any ordinary man or woman in the street would understand the term.

If the SNP are serious about an independent Scotland, the only credible response to Mark Carney's crucial intervention, and the other academic input in this area, is now to propose a separate Scottish currency, even if only as a stepping stone towards joining the Euro.

Of course, if you believe, as the great majority of people in Scotland do, that we should retain the pound sterling as our currency, there is one very simple way in which to achieve that beyond any doubt, and that is to vote No in the Referendum in September. It is that simple.

What's the point?

Brian Monteith
31 January 2014

I am tempted to say, Game Over. On Wednesday the Governor of the Bank of England, a Canadian of great achievement, supreme technical knowledge and imperious judgement – certainly by comparison with the likes of Alex Salmond, John Swinney, George Osbourne or Ed Balls – came to Edinburgh and gave a dispassionate speech that laid waste the SNP's arguments about an independent Scotland keeping the pound.

Let me be quite precise. Governor Carney did not say an independent Scotland retaining the pound Sterling was impossible. He explained that if that is what his political masters decided – by negotiation between Westminster (his bosses) and Holyrood (his potential clients) then technically it would be feasible.

Nobody challenges this, for its is as true as night follows day. If Westminster agrees to a currency union then it can and will happen.

Nor did Governor Carney make any pronouncement about the pros and cons of Scotland being independent or staying in partnership with the rest of the UK. He studiously avoided taking sides.

All the more then that his technical clarifications were a hammer blow to the SNP vision that everything will be all right on the night, that independence will mean nothing really changes.

Governor Carney made it perfectly clear that if there is to be a currency union using the pound – which means the pound sterling will be the legal tender by which we conduct our trade, pay our wages and settle our debts from John O'Groats to Lands End (as we do now) – then it will require any Scottish government with its new-found independence to give up a significant amount of freedom that it had just won.

The question he provoked was simply this: What's the point?

Before I answer this most obvious of questions let me put a few myths to the sword.

The first is that Scottish banknotes are not legal tender. Much as I love them they are nothing more than marketing ploys to promote the three Scottish banks that are in all circumstances owned by either British or Australian shareholders. In the case of the Royal Bank of Scotland and Bank of Scotland they are actually owned by the UK taxpayer – which means the majority share is English!

The Scottish banknotes are mere affectations of the banks that give us a sense of identity. They are only possible because the banks purchase the equivalent value of Bank of England notes before releasing their own notes into circulation. No person is, however, legally obliged to accept them as tender in any part of Britain, not even in Scotland. That we do, and that some apocryphal London taxi drivers do not, is simply a matter of personal choice.

If an independent Scotland manages to negotiate retaining the pound Sterling as its currency the Scottish banknotes will become as worthless in the UK as the Irish pound was after 1922 – except in a few Irish nationalist bars in north London.

This of course may not matter to those people that never go south of Berwick or Gretna, fair enough, but let's not pretend current circumstances will persist – they will be appreciably worse.

The second myth is that a Scottish Government will be able to influence its own economy to the extent that any independent country with its own currency would be expected to do. After all, surely the point of independence is to act in Scotland's interests and not worry about unemployment in Merseyside or property inflation in Guildford?

There will be no independent Scottish currency, it will be a common currency and that means the levers that influence it – the issuing of debt, notes and coins and the setting of interest rates and taxes – will be set by a committee that is in the UK's favour by a ratio of at least 9/1.

If the price of oil goes up and creates inflationary pressures in Scotland's oil dominated economy (as would be expected) then the interest rates to fight that pressure would not go up – because the deflationary pressures of expensive oil in England would require interest rates to go down. The result would be the wrong interest rates for Scotland creating an economic bubble that would cause great distress when it explodes.

This is precisely what happened to Ireland from being in the Euro during its inflating property bubble. The Germans reduced interest rates when Ireland required higher interest rates. The result was mass Irish unemployment and real wages cut by over 10 per cent. It is a recipe for disaster.

Why seek independence only to then give it up? In fact Scotland – without any access to political influence at Westminster will have less authority in managing the pound Sterling after independence than it has now. After independence politicians will only look to the English not the UK electorate.

Thank you Governor Carney. The question was simple. What's the point? The answer is as easy. Without a separate Scottish Groat there's no point at all.

How Scotland could lose the EU rebate

Ben Acheson
3 February 2014

YES OR NO? Stay or Go? #BetterTogether or #YesScotland? Either way, the #indyref showdown is fast approaching.

The White Paper has come and gone. It was aesthetically pleasing, spruced up with pretty pictures and slick visualisations, but it was dangerously devoid of substance. It was full of contradictory conjecture and groundless reassurances, riddled with inconsistencies and astoundingly short on answers. Its 649 pages detailing the path to independence were ultimately lacking in, well, details.

In one chapter, it claimed that *"successive Westminster Governments have failed to provide effective stewardship of Scotland's oil and gas resources"*. Strange then, that a few paragraphs later, the phrases *"through the success of the last five decades"* and *"international oil and gas centre of excellence"* could be found.

Let's not digress into White Paper bashing though, plenty of others have excoriated it already. The point is that Scotland's monumental decision is on the horizon and too many crucial questions remain unanswered. The entire independence debate is suffocated by over-simplification, romanticism and 'Braveheart'

139

politics. The nitty-gritty details are too often overlooked, assumed to be inconsequential, particularly in discussions about an independent Scotland's EU status.

The future of a nation cannot be decided on conjecture and supposition alone. We need answers.

Admittedly, not all questions can be answered at present. Nobody, from the independence-obsessed to the EU-boffins to the politically ambivalent, can provide a legally-binding answer about Scotland's transition to the EU. Even the European Commission repeatedly affirms that it will only express an opinion on the legal consequences under EC law *'upon request from a Member State detailing a precise scenario'*.

One thing that is clear is that an independent Scotland, as a member of the EU or not, would lose the 'special arrangements' that the UK has negotiated with the EU since joining in 1973. These include an opt-out from the single currency, an opt-out from the Schengen agreement and the provision of the UK rebate. Jose Manuel Barroso, President of the European Commission, confirmed that the special arrangements would remain in place for the UK, but there is universal agreement that they would have to be renegotiated for Scotland.

If you didn't know already, this would be costly.

While the potential costs associated with the two opt-outs have already received considerable media attention, the provision of the rebate has been subject to less analysis. This is because not many people know too much about it and it isn't a 'sexy' media topic which sells papers.

The rebate was first negotiated by Margaret Thatcher in 1984. It was introduced as a redistributive mechanism to address the imbalance between the UK's high contributions to the EU budget and its relatively low economic output. The UK's rebate is the only permanent EU budgetary adjustment; Germany, the Netherlands, Austria and Sweden all have similar mechanisms but they have to constantly renegotiate them.

In practice, the rebate means that around 66 per cent of the UK's net contribution to the EU budget is returned to the UK Government. Instead of the UK simply contributing less, other EU member states, even the newest and the poorest, give money back to the UK. In 2012, the rebate totalled £3.2bn. As it is allocated to the UK Treasury as a lump sum, Scotland does not receive its own rebate. It receives a 'share' of the UK rebate. In 2012, this was around £295 million.

It is a no-brainer that an independent Scotland would not inherit the UK's rebate terms. It would have to negotiate its own. Whether it could be negotiated or not is where the argument lies. Nicola Sturgeon, Deputy Leader of the SNP, claimed that she *"would be confident of an independent Scottish government negotiating a good deal for Scotland"* and the White Paper, while admitting that it would have to be negotiated, asserts that Scotland would eventually inherit the rebate.

False.

What they conveniently forgot to tell us is that the current UK rebate is a major point of contention between the UK and other EU member states. It provokes fierce debate in Brussels. It is widely opposed outside of our borders. Understandably, other EU member states loathe giving vast sums of money to a rich and powerful member state which is increasingly intransigent and reluctant to engage constructively in EU politics. Furthermore, according to recent research, all other EU member states would gain financially from Scotland losing the rebate, with the biggest winners being France (€110m) and Italy (€85m). So why would they agree to let Scotland inherit the UK rebate?

They wouldn't and they won't. The chances that a deal beneficial to Scotland would be reached are slim to none.

If it happened today, the loss of the rebate would mean a direct loss of about £295m (€354m) per annum to Scotland. However, as the UK's rebate would not have to be renegotiated, Scotland, if accepted as a new EU member state, would also have to contribute to financing the UK's rebate. Danny Alexander, Chief Treasury Secretary, recently confirmed that taxpayers in an independent Scotland would end up subsiding England's rebate and recent research published by New Direction showed that Scotland would likely be required to pay between £39m (€47m) and £46m (€55m) to do so.

Adding direct and indirect costs together, the suggestion is that Scotland could directly lose approximately €409m. According to New Direction, these costs would then result in reduced funds available for Scottish Government expenditure, or higher taxes. The sum costs of €409m would then result in a fall in output of €736m and 6,680 jobs foregone.

Those figures relate to the rebate alone. If Scotland had to join the Schengen area with other new member states, border controls with the rest of the UK could cost a further £105 million (€126m). If Scotland was forced to join the euro – as all new member states are currently obliged to do – the total losses from higher transaction costs and changes in trade patterns could cost the Scottish economy up to £468million (€562) per annum. Combined, the £914million (€1,097m) cost of losing all three opt-outs could result in nearly £1.5billion (€1.8bn) of lost output and 17,000 jobs across the Scottish economy.

So Nicola, is this what you meant by *"a good deal for Scotland"*?

Unsurprisingly, the section outlining Scotland's potential EU membership is particularly confusing. Even Salmond himself seems to make it up as he goes along. We have already seen him brazenly inform the President of the European Commission about the EU's own procedures, which backfired when it transpired that Salmond had lied about getting legal advice. He also made unjustifiable claims about timeframes for an independent state becoming a full EU member.

Negotiating with the EU takes years. It is a constant process. There will be no special arrangements for Scotland just because it was part of an existing member state. As Jose Manuel Barroso has repeatedly affirmed, *"if there is a new state, of course, that state has to apply for membership and negotiate the conditions with other member states. For European Union purposes, from a legal point of view, it is certainly a new state. If a country becomes independent it is a new state and has to negotiate with the EU."*

What it means is that the UK would still have its special arrangements with the EU that it has negotiated over the years. Namely,

There has been much discussion about these three issues within the independence debate. Salmond has claimed that Scotland would continue its currency Union with the UK, despite being told repeatedly that any new EU member state must use the Euro. The Schengen agreement has also been scrutinised, but more so to argue about a potential UK-Scotland border.

Additionally, José Manuel Barroso, President of the European Commission, is on record as stating that:

"The EU is founded on the Treaties which apply only to the Member States who have agreed and ratified them. If part of the territory of a Member State would cease to be a part of that state because it were to become a new independent state, the Treaties would no longer apply to that territory. In other words, a new independent state would, by the fact of its independence, become a third country with respect to the EU and the Treaties would no longer apply on its territory."

What Barroso is implying is that Scotland would have to start afresh as a Member State of the EU. Thus, it would be unlikely to continue to receive a rebate.

Why have so few read the White Paper?

James Corbett
4 February 2014

THIS WEEKEND, we had the latest in a long, long line of polls about the independence referendum. The poll, commissioned by Sir Tom Hunter, suggested that there was a slight movement towards "Yes", which has naturally got the Yes campaign crowing about how successful their campaign is. Personally, if I were a Yes supporter, I'd be asking, after all the effort that's been put in, and all the money that's been spent, why the movement is so small?

In any case, that wasn't the most interesting feature of this poll. If the numbers are to be believed then almost a third of Scots haven't heard of the Scottish Government's white paper "Scotland's Future" and of those that have, only 14 per cent have actually looked at it. Even if you give this poll a seriously big margin of error, those numbers should strike fear into the hearts of the nationalists and perhaps Better Together as well.

Given that the White Paper was launched with gigantic fanfare and blanket media coverage, for almost a third of Scots to be unaware of its existence speaks volumes about just how severe the level of political disengagement has become among much of the population.

It's not a complete surprise I suppose. With Holyrood election turnout stuck stubbornly around the 50 per cent mark, there was always going to be a section of the population that just didn't care about the outcome of the independence referendum. Admittedly it's probably wrong to assume that just because someone hasn't heard of the white paper, they don't plan to vote in the referendum, but so many people with a total lack of knowledge of a key component of the Yes camp's argument should be a worry for everyone. If people aren't listening to Yes Scotland, there's no certainty that they're paying any more attention to Better Together.

I've always harboured a suspicion that the white paper could come back to haunt the SNP. That only 14 per cent of those who've heard of the white paper have bothered to read it is curious, particularly when you hear that it's now on it's third reprinting. The only conclusion I can draw is that a large number of the people picking up copies of Scotland's Future are trying to get a souvenir of the debate rather than an insight into it. I'm sure most people wouldn't be interested, but copies of Scotland's Future are for sale on ebay for over £20.

In hindsight, the Scottish Government may come to regret providing hard copies of the document to the public free of charge when the final bill comes in. Although I'd imagine that particular number might not surface until after the referendum.

Apathy in the independence debate is probably more of a concern for Better Together who have the sometimes difficult task of convincing people of the merits of voting not to do something. Most of Yes Scotland's supporters are those who have been committed to independence from the beginning and so are almost certain to all cast a vote. Something that may benefit them if there is a lower turnout.

Wider political apathy, however, is a long-running problem and, despite what some in the Yes campaign might say, it's not going to be cured by voting for independence.

Whether Scotland is an independent country or part of the UK, it will still have the same long standing problems it has now. I say "long standing problems" very deliberately as there's been a tendency by nationalists to encourage a Yes vote on the basis of opposition to unpopular policies pursued by current and previous Westminster governments. An unpopular policy like the bedroom tax (or whatever you want to call it) can be undone by a change of government rather than a change of constitution. There's no similarly simple fix for the biggest problems in our society. Although, if I understand Alex Neil, the invention of a time machine and the assassination of Margaret Thatcher would solve Scotland's alcohol and drug abuse problems.

Political apathy and bad politics form a vicious circle. The less people care about politics, the fewer people choose to engage with it. The fewer people engaging with politics, the less diverse and representative the views within the political arena become. The less representative the views, the less people are driven to care enough to vote on them.

However much the nationalists might talk of Scotland gaining economic levers (subject to the approval of Mark Carney) and full decision making powers for the Scottish Parliament through independence, it's meaningless if the people making the decisions don't use them wisely. Wherever the powers to decide Scotland's future lie after the 18th of September, politicians need to find ways to get the public to re-engage with politics or the future of Scotland is going to be one that the majority of people won't have chosen.

First Minister Jim Sillars anyone?

The referendum: forward, blindfolded, into the voting booth

Bill Jamieson
5 February 2014

A WARNING by Bob Dudley, boss of oil giant BP, about breaking away from the rest of the UK rightly has rightly grabbed the headlines and given lead story treatment on the BBC for most of yesterday.

The 'Yes' campaign might well feel a sense of relief that the coverage of Mr Dudley's remarks has done it a favour.

For the head of the North Sea's biggest investor was not the only one to pipe up on the independence question. Blanket coverage of his remarks that the UK was best to stay together *masked two other* significant statements yesterday.

Owen Kelly, head of Scottish Financial Enterprise, gave a forthright public warning that Scotland's £11 billion fund management industry employing 100,000 directly would face a multi-million pound bill to pay for a new financial regulator if independence went ahead.

He told the *Financial Times* yesterday that "a yes vote would require the creation of an additional financial regulator with

149

hundreds of staff. The cost would run into millions and have to be paid for by the industry in Scotland.

"Some changes will be necessary if fund managers cease to be in the same legal jurisdiction as the City of London and 90 per cent of their customers."

Adrian Cammidge, head of communications at Edinburgh-based Kames Capital, said: 'We have a significant majority of customers outside of Scotland and a clear duty of care to ensure they are not disadvantaged by a Yes vote.'

Familiar? You read this here just two weeks ago when I warned that, "with around 90 per cent of Scottish financial sector business generated outside of Scotland, institutional and private clients alike will need every assurance on how regulation might work. Will there be extra costs for the industry with Scotland setting up its own regulator, and to which regulatory authority would firms be answerable? Concern over both tax and currency risk could not only act as a deterrent for rUK clients but could also see a withdrawal of funds. Unless full safeguards and guarantees are given, Scotland could see one of its key sectors melt away before its eyes."

As if all this was not enough, two senior retail experts yesterday reignited the row over the prospect of grocery prices rising after independence. Justin King, chief executive of Sainsburys, joined the bosses of ASDA and Morrisons in warning of higher prices in a separate Scotland. He told the FT: "Once it is a separate country, we and other retailers will take a view of what the cost structure is of that industry, and of course the revenue structure too. If you were to strike that today, there is no doubt Scotland is a more costly country [in which] to run a grocery retail business."

And John Fingleton, former chair of the Irish Competition Authority and former chief executive of the UK's Office of Fair Trading told the paper, "If those costs are isolated to Scotland only, it will just push up the prices in Scotland and lower prices in England. All of the retail sectors where in-time distribution matters [will be looking at this]."

All this came hard on the heels of a stinging paper this week by the Institute of Chartered Accountants of Scotland. It fired no less than 35 questions the Scottish government has still to answer on how pensions would be administered, funded and maintained in an independent Scotland including:

• Who would make State pension payments in an independent Scotland and take responsibility for any entitlements built up prior to independence?

• What State pension arrangements would the Scottish Government need to introduce? What transitional arrangements would be needed?

• What would the Scottish Government receive, if anything, from the UK Government by way of providing for those of working age with "accrued" entitlement to a State pension?

Arcane and esoteric matters of only marginal interest? The ICAS paper points out that as at 31 March 2012, the UK government reported unfunded public sector pension liabilities of £919 billion. What would Scotland's share be in the opening balance sheet of an independent Scotland? For schemes that are Scottish based, the Scottish Public Pensions Agency has recently identified unfunded liabilities of £60 billion representing 70 per cent of Scottish public sector pension liabilities identified so far. However, work still has to be done to identify additional liabilities relating to Scottish-based members of UK-wide public sector pension schemes.

Affordability, ICAS notes, is a challenge for many developed countries including the UK, "but the demographics of Scotland with a higher projected ratio of pensioners to those of working age population mean that this is likely to be more of a challenge here." Even setting aside last week's speech by Bank of England Governor Mark Carney on the fiscal and monetary constraints a shared currency would impose on an independent Scotland, each of these interventions raises important issues on which voters deserve clarity. Together they pose a major challenge to the credibility of the independence case.

And they demand a more serious response than dismissive comments about being "personal remarks" or "technical issues" or the fall-back knee-jerk riposte about "Project Fear". If that's all we're going to get from Alex Salmond and the SNP it is being more than evasive. It is asking Scots to walk blindfold into the voting booth on the biggest constitutional question put before them.

The SNP has no new ideas for a Scottish NHS

Jonathan Stanley
7 February 2014

HEALTHCARE is one of the single largest costs to the economy, both in Scotland and the UK, currently at around 9 per cent of GDP, yet the omission of detail over how healthcare could be delivered by a separate Scotland is astounding. Beyond mentioning that we'd have "the full range of levers to promote good health" there is little of substance.

Four paragraphs are devoted to dismissing concerns over cross-border logistics and payments for transplant patients before ascending into blue sky, cherry pie country by explaining that while the NHS currently operates within a UK framework for negotiating pay, that post 2016 the, "machinery would be reviewed...with potential for improvement across Scotland". In terms of primary and secondary care and long term issues of pay and pensions the SNP either believes devolution works perfectly well or it hasn't a scooby on how it could be done differently.

Despite a plethora of healthcare models across the OECD to choose from and EU directives on cross-border provision of healthcare in the mix, the SNP strides to avoid competition that, in absence of elected health boards, puts all decisions on healthcare provision squarely in the hands of MSPs, few of whom have ever worked in the health service.

If only the First Minister had used more of his crayons to outline reforms to general practice to suit patients with inflexible working times, to commit to redressing dubious PFI projects that cripple the NHS in Lothian and Lanarkshire, or review targets without evidence base brought in by Labour, there could be some hope that the SNP's view of healthcare in Scotland would be less a "Little Britain" and more a centre of excellence where patient choice, clinical excellence and popular sovereignty leads the NHS.

The 1990s saw a big push by Labour to win office and a concerted effort was made in campaigning in Labour's natural strengths; including the NHS. Health boards have been crippled by PFI debts that the SNP opposed but never redressed. Despite this folly of central planning the nationalists view of healthcare has become ever more centralised around political bodies and universal targets that go against the grain of equitable treatment based on need. This was a cornerstone of the NHS in Scotland that the left has casually tossed aside.

One target that has caused concern and has politicised an entire clinical specialty is the four hour Accident and Emergency waiting target. It must be singly the most overtly political, divisive and wasteful target in the history of hospital medicine. We praise a system where a broken toe is treated as quickly as a broken leg and patients can choose to wait days for an appointment that costs pounds or jump the queue by attending A&E where a refusal to treat is as rare as kelpie manure and treatment within four hours is mandatory.

The result is extreme waste compounded by out-of-hours GPs working in separate locations to A&E departments. When patients are unsure how ill they really are, moral hazard again kicks in and patients with bumps on the head, a lump in the neck for two weeks fight for the attentions and affections of overworked junior doctors with the eternally anxious heart attack patients, stroke victims and those with severe pneumonia.

This equality of treatment means *equitable treatment* is nigh impossible and the most vulnerable are the first and worst to suffer. A&Es should not be a catch-all solution, nor is it enough to simply ask GPs to see more and more patients with very little acutely wrong with them. NHS Scotland should allow health boards to set waiting times according to clinical triaging systems which have a strong evidence base.

There are many demand side and supply side solutions that could be applied yet we should accept A&Es are hubs, not terminal destinations, and that the back end of patient flow is often beyond the department's control. Improved patient flow schemes like the one developed by the Northern General Hospital in Sheffield should be applied across Scotland and NHS X-prizes should be offered to clinical teams at the coal face who produce such innovative solutions.

Drunk tanks for those who are drunk but otherwise well would discourage the use of hospitals as bed and breakfasts for the irresponsible and hotel fees could dissuade many from abusing a free service. *Hotel fees are well known and accepted across Scandinavia so the SNP need not be feart of considering them.* In any case being drunk and disorderly or even incapable are criminal offences and health boards should be free to recover costs in full, with discounts for those with an addiction that they accept treatment for. Those with money for booze have money to lose and it is better to charge people for reckless drinking than try to punish everyone with minimum alcohol charging.

Advanced paramedics in the south of England, and doctors in Germany, drive out to cases triaged by paramedics with experience, not silly computer algorithms, to determine if a patient really needs an ambulance. Real time assessment of need by professionals will be more acceptable to patients than charging for ambulances for all but the very worst offenders and force the NHS to move away from the idea that the patient revolves around the provider: the opposite must be the case.

There is no honest reason to keep patients who are normally well and working fenced in by a single GP practice. These people essentially never need home visits yet time spent off work can be very detrimental to their finances and careers. Unbundling primary care services can mean a few practices developing a tailored range of services to suit this group, with at least one evening session a week and the opportunity to allow top-up payments for patients who want discrete treatment by a named GP outside normal hours.

Out of hours GP services should be co-located with A&E and be accessed post-triage so patients can be both reassured of the non-urgency of their case but then be seen by an appropriate level provider before the condition deteriorates. This is especially important for worried parents of small children and babies and these measures present a real chance for the right to fight for the concerns of young and working families. The problem is, all of these policies could be enacted right now, in a Scotland within the UK, and that may of course be the problem.

Scotland's Future cites several major achievements in healthcare yet none of these can be attributed to a specific Scottish policy or extend beyond managerial and bureaucratic tinkering of a healthcare system increasing at odds with the mainstream in Europe and Australasia. We will ignore, for now, that waiting times in NHS Lothian have been completely fudged and that the SNP's paternalist obsession with smoking in public is tokenism more aimed at legitimising state control over the individual than delivering real gains in health for the Scottish people.

Scotland's Future is a damning indictment of the centralising statist mindset of the SNP that flirts between cherishing the Labour planned, Westminster-led *status quo* and the vaguest havering of a better future, with a dearth of detail either way.

It's about family, not finances

Brian Monteith
7 February 2014

Those storms down in Devon and Cornwall look atrocious and I feel for the people on the telly, almost nightly, being forced to move out of their once safe, dry homes to a place of refuge. The same goes for the people in Somerset with those floods that seem to have been with them longer than the rains that caused the ark to be built.

To me, they are my fellow countrymen and women. To me they are family; their suffering is my suffering, their joy is my joy, their success is my success, and although we may from time to time be in competition with each other – like Edinburgh can be in competition with Glasgow – I know that in the scheme of things we are all working to make a better place of our island nation.

We get far more by baking a bigger pie than fighting over the share of the existing pie, that is meanwhile likely to go stale.

Regular readers of this column will know that I get around a bit. As a traveller I do not think I am unusual when I say that in the years I worked in London I found myself more patriotically Scottish and missing Auld Reekie than when I was in Edinburgh. I shall never forget being at Twickenham to see Scotland beat

England in 1983. Although I developed a liking for hoppy English ales I would seek out Scottish beers and single malts and champion them whenever I found them.

Similarly, when I was in Pakistan, Trinidad or Botswana I was often nostalgic and patriotic towards Britain and the British way of life. I never visit a country without meeting people that are warm to me because I am British, that love our cultural heritage from Kipling to Kelman or the Beatles to Burns, that admire the laws we left behind or the opportunities Great Britain has given them or their families.

I've met Germans that have thanked me for the work of Britons in drawing up their constitution; Icelanders from the President down that have benefited from our universities, Nigerians that have lived and prospered due to our delivering of vital utilities – often on occasions when others would not help.

When we were together us ex-pats liked to make jokes at each others expense and laugh at ourselves, it was part of our humour that the locals often found odd and unrecognisable amongst themselves. A colleague from Leeds might introduce me to clients as like a Yorkshireman but without a sense of humour – I would respond and introduce him as like a Scotsman but without any generosity! Later I would use the same joke with an Aberdonian as we would again rib each other.

And when I have worked, lived and holidayed in all parts of the United Kingdom – and these days maybe too many of us rush to go to Spain or other warmer climes before getting to know our own country – I have always found Scots or husbands and wives or sons and daughters of Scots in the smallest nook and cranny as if they had always been there. Some three hundred years ago that would have been thought of as highly unusual, dangerous even. Now it is commonplace, so much so that it's taken for granted.

The fabric of Great Britain is rich and beautiful, it is a tartan tweed jacket with blood stains and beer stains and leather patches on the elbows. It occasionally needs a repair, maybe a clean but it at once protective and warm in the cold and cool and airy in the heat. If it were to lose a sleeve that was then only pinned back on, or worse, stuffed in the pocket, it would be less than the sum of its parts.

I retell these experiences because it is very easy to think that all the debate about Scotland's future in the United Kingdom is about currency, pensions, supermarket prices, border controls, interest rates and the general standard of living or swallow the racist conceit of some nationalists who like to suggest that English folk are Dickensian John Bulls wanting the poor in the workhouse and immigrants sent packing.

So this week when we heard from three Scots economic professors that an independent Scotland could suffer twenty-five years of hardship; or from the highly successful chief executive of Sainsbury's that grocery prices in a separate Scotland were bound to be higher; or from the Scottish accountants' body that the future of Scottish pensions was unknown; I raised only two cheers for them making everyone aware of the issues at stake.

What I reserved three cheers for was when the Chief Executive of BP, Bob Dudley, waded in to the debate – not because he said his company's investment might be at risk but because he said "Great Britain is Great" – for it is not said enough. It is not the bean-counting that will sway the majority of people about how they vote, it is how they feel about continuing to be British in a closer way than independence will ever allow. It's about creating and spreading opportunities and the sharing of risks. Being in Great Britain gives us more and it will cost us less.

Different countries? Or just wishful thinking?

Murdo Fraser

8 February 2014

IN HIS famous book "Democracy in America", the 19th century French statesman and theorist Alexis de Tocqueville observed that "the manners of the people may be considered as one of the great general causes to which the maintenance of a democratic republic in the United States is attributable". De Tocqueville's theory was that commonly held beliefs, for example on freedom of religion, were what underpinned American democracy. This enabled government to function without oppression of the masses, as had been the case in his native France (and elsewhere in per centEurope) in the previous centuries.

It has become a generally accepted principle that successful democratic countries do require a population that holds certain values in common. Bitter divisions, whether these be related to wealth, social status, or views on race, undermine good and peaceful government. Ultimately, they may cause social unrest or even disintegration.

Against this backdrop, it is not surprising that the argument used by many of those campaigning for a separate Scotland is that people here hold different attitudes to those in the rest of the UK, and particularly in England. We see this as a running theme in any comments made by SNP politicians and others in the Yes campaign. Scotland is, supposedly, more socially democratic, more left-wing, and generally "nicer" than right-leaning, anti-immigrant, Euro-sceptic, UKIP-voting England.

There is nothing new in Scottish nationalists holding these views. In a famous speech at Glasgow University in 1968, the self-confessed Anglophobic writer Hugh MacDiarmid said "there are not two nations under the firmament that are more contrary and different from each other than Englishmen and Scotsmen, how be it they be within one island, and neighbours, and of one language. For Englishmen are subtle and Scotsmen are facile, Englishmen are ambitious in prosperity and Scotsmen are humane in prosperity, Englishmen are humble when they are subdued by force and violence, and Scotsmen are furious when they are violently subdued. Englishmen are cruel when they get victory, and Scotsmen are merciful when they get victory. It is impossible that Scotsmen and Englishmen can remain in concord under one government because their nature and conditions are as different as is the nature of sheep and wolves..." Fortunately most of those involved in today's Yes campaign would eschew such racist utterances, but we can still see echoes of MacDiarmid's words in the current debate.

I have written previously about "the myth of Scots moral superiority", arguing that, contrary to the separatists' claims, evidence would suggest that we are much closer in thinking to our English neighbours than many would assert. Further evidence has appeared in recent weeks in support of this view.

For example, the Social Attitudes Survey found that there was growing Euro-scepticism in Scotland. In 2003 40 per cent of Scots wanted Britain to either leave the EU, or see a reduction in powers. This now stands at 60 per cent (63 per cent of No voters and 57 per cent of Yes voters).

When it comes to welfare, 56 per cent of No voters and 46 per cent Yes voters think unemployment benefits are too high and discourage people from finding a job. And on immigration, 77 per cent of respondents across the UK said that it should be reduced, whilst in Scotland the figure was 69 per cent, and 47 per cent across Britain said immigration affected the economy badly, whilst in Scotland the equivalent figure was 44 per cent.

So little evidence there that Scots are substantially to the left of people in England in terms of their outlook on political issues, and certainly nothing to suggest that we are the "different country" in terms of views that some in the separatist camp would claim.

There have been two further straws in the wind which should not be ignored. For years we have been told by nationalists that UKIP's failure to make any political progress in Scotland, whilst polling on occasion well into the teens in England, is another illustration of how divergent our political systems have become.

I have pointed out before that one of the principle reasons why UKIP does not do so well in Scotland is that, as an anti-establishment nationalistic party with a charismatic and media-savvy leader, UKIP finds that that territory is already occupied in Scotland by the SNP.

But even having said that, UKIP appear, slowly, to be making some ground. In the recent Cowdenbeath by-election, despite losing her deposit, the UKIP candidate finished in fourth place, ahead of the Lib Dems. And a poll of voting intentions for the forthcoming Euro elections showed UKIP again in fourth place, again beating the Lib Dems, although likely to fall short of winning one of the six Scottish seats up for grabs.

Different countries? Certainly there are differences in outlook, and differences in voting patterns. But I suspect that if Alexis de Tocqueville were alive today and travelling throughout the United Kingdom, he would find the customs of the people varying little from one end to the other.

Greater freedom should be our call as we defend the Union

Andrew Morrison
10 February 2014

I AM, at a basic level, a supporter of the concept of Better Together and believe nationally it is doing more good than harm for our campaign to remain within the UK. Yes, some activists may complain about local difficulties such as poor communication with other parties, resentment that others are not pulling their weight, or expressing desire to divert more resources to their party interests instead, but in the bigger picture as a campaign vehicle and as an organisation flagging up the fundamental flaws in the Yes campaign it is working well.

There was always going to be weaknesses attached to an organisation underpinned by three political parties which hold fundamentally different views on what constitutes good governance.

That is why I also support the idea that Labour and Conservatives have their own vehicles, such as *United With Labour* and the *Conservative Friends of the Union*. It makes common sense in so far as the political parties have their own

165

campaign spending limits to utilise in conjunction with the Better Together spending limit, and it is right the political parties have their own organisations to raise funds to maximise their spending allowances. That ultimately benefits us all.

Setting finances aside though, when you bring together three different visions for what Scotland's future within the United Kingdom should constitute, we basically have a Venn diagram. For the Better Together campaign to continue to be as coherent as it has been to date, it is restricted to setting out policy positions slap bang in the middle where the three parties congregate e.g. currency, defence, security, border control, broadcasting, the desire for growth within our current model as compared to, say, a radical change in our economic system.

As a Conservative through and through, I have to say I want our party to use this campaign as a springboard for our own interests also. The Conservative Friends of the Union has been successful at doing this.

But I think it is about time we started to express more conservative principals and core values in our argument for remaining within the United Kingdom. This is a time when the Scottish public are engaging with politics in a way they haven't done so for many years. A significant number of people I know who generally do not vote – and a handful who have never voted, ever – are aware of the campaign and the main thrust of the arguments being made on both sides.

I want my Party to express our core values during the course of this argument while Scotland is paying attention to what our politicians are saying.

The Prime Minister's speech last week was very heavy on the emotional argument – and that is not to be neglected – however with polls indicating a difference of £500 making a substantial difference to voting intentions, we mustn't neglect the logical, rational argument neither. David Cameron notably omitted this from his case for a No vote.

Somewhere in this debate there is space for us to say 'yes, Conservatives support freedom – freedom for the people, not Scotland from the UK'. We'd reinstate the freedom to buy your home, give more people the support they need to have the freedom to set up their own businesses. We support the freedom that employment brings, hence why we've been supporting the long term unemployed back into work whereas the SNP have opposed every single penny piece of the welfare reforms led by the Conservatives at Westminster.

It is about time Conservative representatives started to speak up. Yes, we believe in independence, but a meaningful type of independence.

Give people more independence from the state, not Scotland independence from the UK, and we'll deliver a more meaningful type of freedom that will truly benefit peoples' day to day lives. Concentrate our efforts on giving the people more freedom, because it is people, the businesses they run, and third sector organisations they are involved in which will make Scotland a better nation. Not the State. This is not the 1930s where the State had discretion over the public utilities, incomes, prices, rents, etc.

When it really boils down to it, it is people who make Scotland what is. It is Scottish people and the businesses they run that put us on the map in the hearts and minds of the people of the world. It is the goods we export, the services we have to offer, our innovations, the type of people we are at home and abroad, that define us as a nation – not where we choose to govern ourselves from.

As the only centre-right political party in Scotland, if we do not make this case, who will? And if we do not make this case now when the country is paying some degree of attention, then when will we make it?

Will independence mean no more Tory governments?

Brian Monteith
10 February 2014

There are many tartan kites flown by the SNP in an attempt to garner more Yes votes; these include that Scotland can keep the pound without losing it's newly-gained economic independence, that we can have different immigration policies to encourage its plan for 100,000 incomers without it resulting in border controls from Berwick to Gretna, that we can maintain the beneficial social union with the rest of Britain whilst they mock its people as being mean, prejudiced and small-minded – while charging its sons and daughters to study here.

There is, however, a greater deceit that it is repeatedly flaunted, especially when the Prime Minister dares to comment about the value of Scotland being inside the United Kingdom, and that is that there will never again be Tory governments in power in Scotland. Whether it be Alex Salmond or his deputy Nicola Sturgeon that accuses the Prime Minister of being the "embodiment" of the case for independence, the message is clear: just vote Yes and Conservatives will never again rule in Scotland.

This is a bit rich coming from a First Minister whose minority government relied upon the political support of Annabel Goldie when she was leader of the Scottish Conservatives, but it also ignores Scottish and international history which supplies ample evidence that an independent Scotland might expect to have Tory rulers within a generation.

Nationalists are in the habit of looking east towards Scandinavia for examples of how Scotland might be, not just because it provides some examples of a social democratic society that it presents as preferable to our own, but also because it adds to the narrative that nationalists are busy inventing which says the differences between Scotland and England are greater than the similarities. What is conveniently forgotten is that all Scandinavian governments have elected what might be called Tory governments in modern times and (this is the sweetly ironic part) especially so since Margaret Thatcher established what is described by her critics as a neo-liberal economic consensus in Western Europe.

This week John Swinney visits Norway and the opportunity is not being lost to suggest we could be more like the Norwegians. What is not being said is that its conservative party, Høyre, has formed governments on eight occasions since liberation from the German occupation in 1945 and leads the current ruling coalition government with Conservative Erna Solberg as Prime Minister.

Iceland, that erstwhile member of Alex Salmond's "arc of Prosperity" has seen conservative prime ministers from its Independence Party lead seventeen of its thirty-one administrations since 1945, more than either the Progressive or Social Democrat parties. Even when other parties have provided the premier the Independence Party has often been a member of the ruling coalition, as is currently the case.

The Conservative Peoples Party in Denmark might on first sight appear to have had a harder time of it, managing to participate in only ten administrations since the War – but it can point to its premier Paul Schlüter forming four governments between 1982 and 1993 and having been in power for twenty-one of the last thirty-two years.

The current prime minister of Finland, Jyrki Katainen, is leader of its conservative party, Kokoomus, and while there has been only one other premier from that party since 1945 it has participated in ten governments and had the largest share of the vote in the 2011 elections.

While Sweden is often presented as famously social democrat it too has had what we would recognise as Conservative Prime Minsters in Carl Bildt (1991-94) and the current incumbent Fredrik Reinfeldt, who has been in power since 2006 – a year longer than Alex Salmond!

Taking a wider view we can see that conservatives are currently part of the ruling governments of every Scandinavian country except Denmark and provide the premier in Sweden, Norway and Finland. Like all conservative parties around the world they differ in some degrees, but all are members of the International Democrat Union along with the British Conservatives, the US Republicans, the Canadian Conservatives and Australia's Liberals.

The Scottish Conservative and Unionist Party can trace its antecedents to the *old* Scottish Parliament and is by any measure Scotland's oldest political party. Were independence to present itself there would be a need for a new centre-right party to form and we know there are some political activists, mostly former Scottish Conservatives, waiting to do this. My old friends Michael Fry and Peter de Vink are two such formidable people, and who is to say they, together with others, would not be able to form a new Scottish political force that would become a member of the IDU?

Are we honestly to believe that socialist or social democrat opponents including the SNP, if it does not break up into different parts, would not call them "same old Tories"? Fry and de Vink are honest and sincere in promoting their own recipe of neo-liberal policies of low taxes (preferably a flat tax), minimal government and an open society – this is pretty much the antithesis of what Nicola Sturgeon, The Jimmy Reid Foundation and many other vocal supporters of nationalism say Scotland will obtain once Scotland is independent.

Do Salmond, Sturgeon et al honestly believe Scottish conservatives of one name or another (undoubtedly they would seek a different brand identity) would not one day be in a position of power, maybe in coalition, even providing the First Minister? It is disingenuous to suggest that through independence there will be no Scottish Tory governments, not only is it a promise the SNP cannot possibly keep, for it will be future electorates that will decide, it is a deceit to suggest it unlikely. It is probably likely at some stage - even if it takes twenty or thirty years to happen.

What I believe some nationalists really want to say – but cannot for fear of being branded racialist bigots – is that there will be no more *English* Tory governments, so they limit themselves to saying no more Tories as a barely concealed code, a euphemism, for their prejudice.

Alex Salmond is either playing Peter de Vink and Michael Fry for fools by encouraging them to promote a free market independent Scotland when he does not want one or believe there will be one – or he and Sturgeon are deceiving the Scottish public when they say independence will rid Scotland of Tory rule. I hope it is the latter. It cannot be both.

Osborne detonates Carney's torpedo

Murdo Fraser

15 February 2014

SOMETIMES, just occasionally, I actually feel sorry for those campaigning for a Yes vote in September's referendum. I have good friends in the SNP, and whilst I fundamentally disagree with them on Scotland's constitutional future, nevertheless I can respect their long-held view that we should be a separate country.

On so many issues, these hard-working and loyal campaigners have been poorly served by the leadership of the Yes Campaign. Nowhere has this become more evident than in the debate over currency options for an independent Scotland, a debate which burst back into flames on Thursday with George Osborne's speech in Edinburgh, and his announcement that, in the event of independence, the rest of the UK would have no interest in a currency union with Scotland. In this, he was backed up by the Treasury spokesman in both Labour and the Liberal Democrats.

So we are left in no doubt, that a currency option across the UK, which is detailed in the White Paper and was the subject of the SNP's "Fiscal Commission" Paper, will not now happen. It will not happen if there is a Conservative government, a Liberal Democrat government, a Labour government, or any combination of the three. It is a dead duck.

Perhaps the most surprising aspect of the reaction to Osborne's speech was that some people were surprised by it at all. Two weeks ago, the Governor of the Bank of England, Mark Carney, made a speech in Edinburgh in which he set out in detail the pros and cons of a currency union. He made quite clear that whilst there would be certain advantages to such an arrangement, there were also substantial disadvantages, particularly to the larger partner.

All the risk in such an arrangement would be borne not by Scotland, but by the rest of the UK, and this created the problem that he identified of a "moral hazard". It was therefore by no means certain that the rest of the UK would see a currency union with Scotland desirable.

Osborne's speech on Thursday took this one step further. Having taken Treasury advice, the Chancellor's (logical and understandable) conclusion was that a currency union would not be in the rest of the UK's interests. It would expose the rest of the UK to too much risk and uncertainty, and would only work in the event that there was a substantial level of political integration across the former UK, which the Scottish people would have signalled by a Yes vote in a referendum that they were no longer prepared to accept.

The Nationalist reaction to Osborne's comments was as laughable as it was lightweight. The Deputy First Minister, Nicola Sturgeon, was left, in the manner of a spoilt two-year-old refusing to accept that it was bedtime, bleating about "bullying and intimidation" by Westminster, completely missing the point that all the Chancellor was indicating was that, post independence, the rest of the UK would take decisions in the best interests of its own citizens, as indeed one would expect the Scottish government to do for its own people.

Not only was this bullying, Miss Sturgeon claimed, it was also bluffing. In the event of a Yes vote, there would be an immediate U-turn, and the government of the rest of the UK would enter a currency union anyway, despite the protestations. But why would they? As Mark Carney pointed out, there are clear downsides to such an arrangement. With such a clear political message at this stage, it is inconceivable that any UK politician could survive such a dramatic U-turn. This was no bluff; it is a position which needs to be taken seriously.

Other Nationalists were even more bizarre in their arguments. On *Newsnight* Scotland on Wednesday evening, the normally fairly sensible Alex Bell tried to argue that refusing a currency union was a breach of the Edinburgh Agreement. Funny that, there is no word whatsoever in the Edinburgh Agreement of currency. What he seemed to be arguing was that a Yes vote meant that the rest of the UK had to sign up to everything the SNP demanded. Well if that is what the Edinburgh Agreement means, then surely that should have been spelt out explicitly? It was patent nonsense.

We then heard that the pound and the Bank of England were 'assets' of the UK, so an independent Scotland would have the right to share them. But, as Professor Adam Tomkins has pointed out, a currency is not an asset as such; it is a means of exchange. And claiming a share in a UK institution such as the Bank of England is as absurd as claiming a share in the House of Lords post-independence.

Having launched all the toys out of the pram, the next Nationalist response was to say that if the pound could not be shared, an independent Scotland would default on its responsibility towards paying the rest of the UK's national debt. This is insanity. Speaking on Newsnight Scotland, Dr Angus Armstrong of NIESR, the academic who knows more than most about currency issues, said rather more politely that such a suggestion was "irresponsible". And it is.

Firstly, refusing to accept any debts would mean Scotland would not be entitled to any share of UK assets. Secondly, it could leave Scotland in the eyes of the international money markets as a pariah state, either not able to borrow money at all, or only borrow it at very high interest rates.

Even without the historic UK debt, the finances of Scotland at present run with an annual £7billion deficit between revenue and expenditure, and the position is projected to deteriorate post 2016. So the government of an independent Scotland has, from day one, to borrow in excess of £500million each and every month simply to pay the bills. Who is going to lend this money, and at what cost?

What this whole episode exposes is how weak the SNP have been on the whole currency issue. We know there is no Plan B for currency, worse than that, now there is no plan at all. A currency union off the table leaves just three options: sterlingisation (using the pound without a currency union), a separate Scottish currency, or joining the Euro.

To deal with the third option first, joining the Euro doesn't work in the short term, partly because we don't meet the convergence criteria, and partly because the rules state that we need to have our own separate currency for at least three years before we can enter. So that leaves us with either a separate currency or sterlingisation.

There are models of a shared currency without a formal currency union elsewhere in the world which work, for example Panama and Hong Kong both use the US Dollar. However, as many academics have pointed out, such arrangements only exist where a country either does not have a large financial sector, or (like Hong Kong) has very low levels of debt and substantial national reserves. As Scotland does not fall into this latter category, and does have a large financial sector, it would present enormous risks.

Sterlingisation means that there would be no central bank in Scotland, and no lender of last resort. There would be no one to stand behind our financial institutions in the event of another economic crisis. That means waving goodbye to RBS, to Standard

Life, to Aberdeen Asset Management, to Alliance Trust, and to a whole host of other financial institutions, who would have no interest in continuing to be based in Scotland without that protection. It would be a disaster for the Scottish economy.

That leaves us with a separate Scottish currency. I have argued before that this is the logical position for an independent Scotland to take. However, it would require a huge amount of preparation and planning, which due to the essential stupidity of SNP strategists will not yet have happened. Moreover, any such currency, if pegged in informal arrangement to the pound, would be vulnerable to international speculators. And it would require a separate Scottish central bank, which again would have the problem of raising funds on the international money markets (substantially more difficult if there had been a default on share of UK debt).

So it is all a mess. To try and retrieve the situation, the SNP need to stop blustering about bullying and bluffing, and come out and tell us what their currency plan now is. Otherwise they will lose the last shreds of credibility that they still retain.

Two weeks ago Mark Carney launched a torpedo at the SNP's currency union plans. Two days ago, George Osborne detonated it. I hope my friends in the SNP survive the scramble for the lifeboats.

There are many positives for being in the UK but our Social Union is possibly the most important

Brian Monteith
17 February 2014

The demand from Yes campaigners for the No campaign to be less negative and offer a positive vision of Scotland's future has been repeated so often that it has now become a tiresome cliché. It is all the more ironic then that the greatest advocates of the positive case for Scotland remaining in the United Kingdom are in fact Yes campaigners and politicians themselves.

We see it all the time by the way advocates of independence define what they mean. We shall retain the Queen as our head of state instead of being offered the choice to become a republic. They say we shall remain members of the European Union instead of being offered the choice to be like Norway, Iceland or Switzerland and limit ourselves to being European trading partners. We shall apply to join Nato to have a mutually assured defence structure that will involve exercises with the RAF, Royal Navy and British Army regiments instead of being neutral and outside any military alliance.

We are still being told we shall have a currency union although it can now be seen that it is absolutely beyond the power of the SNP to deliver it formally. We are also told that we shall maintain our social union despite the fact that charging the thousands of English, Welsh and Northern Irish students for university fees is not only illegal within the EU but is also certain to create a significant grievance in the continuing UK if we do not charge Germans, Greeks or Spaniards the same fees.

We are even told that we shall still be able to watch Eastenders and Coronation Street without the blink of an eye, because arrangements will be put in place to purchase such British productions, just like we pay to watch the English Premiership on Sky or BT already.

So there we have it, being in the United Kingdom has given us many strong and positive advantages. We have a highly stable and well respected constitutional monarchy that provides a reassuring and unifying stability while politicians come and go and fall in and out of fashion.

We have been members of the European Union for some forty years and Nato for more than sixty – bringing openness, economic growth, democracy and security that other nations have aspired to and queued up to join.

Our own common currency provides a means of exchange redeemable throughout the land that suits us better than using a foreign coinage and gives us a flexibility in the world economy that is the envy of so many nations that made the mistake of joining the Euro.

And we have a social union between Scotland and England that after, not just years or decades, but centuries of wars, battles, and bloody invasions (by either side) has encouraged us to migrate, intermingle, forge familial bonds and establish through perseverance and endeavour great successes in commerce, culture, science and politics. There are communities, even towns that are thought of as being essentially Scottish. The extent to which our social union became possible in the United Kingdom, despite further civil wars where Scots themselves were divided, is nowadays taken for granted – just as the huge role we played in establishing what was to become the British Empire and then latterly the Commonwealth, is often forgotten.

Some intentionally provocative and disrespectful nationalists like to call the Union Flag the butchers apron, conveniently avoiding the fact that if there were indeed any butchers they were as likely to be Scots as anyone else. Key events in our British history, such as the Battle of Trafalgar had a disproportionately large number of Scots (over a third) while we all know the names of great Scots who helped shape the modern world – often from their position of influence at the great educational institutions in the metropolis or at Oxford and Cambridge.

The idea we are so subservient, passive and lacking in confidence within our great social union as to be unable to lead men to make the greatest of sacrifices, discover the unknown, develop new ideas, forge new enterprises, build lasting and enviable institutions – and yes, run our country, the United Kingdom of Great Britain and Northern Ireland – because we are Scots and not born to do so is the worst example of the Scottish cringe.

Was I dreaming when that Scottish son of the manse, Gordon Brown, became British Prime Minister and was widely accepted at the time by an English dominated Labour Party? Brown was hardly born to run the country.

Maybe I imagined that Anthony Charles Lynton Blair, that humble bungalow-lad from Paisley Terrace, nestling in the shadow of Arthur's Seat, became the Labour Party's longest-serving prime minister and the only person to lead that party to three consecutive general election victories. He was hardly born to run the UK. The second son of Leo, an illegitimate child of two English actors who was adopted and raised by a Glaswegian shipyard worker James Blair. Such are the blood lines of our social union that has seen Scotsmen and women go on through their own endeavour to achieve great things and be accepted north and south of the old border.

Is it also not true that a Scot, Alistair Darling, followed Brown as Chancellor, that the late Robin Cook was Foreign Secretary and that George Robertson and John Reid all held high cabinet rank – along with many other Scots? Would John Smith – that Dunoon Grammar School lad not have become prime minister but for his untimely death in 1994?

Then let us not forget Edinburgh's George Watson's lad Malcolm Rifkind, hewn from Jewish Lithuanian immigrant stock – hardly a traditional Scottish background, but rising to become Foreign Secretary and Defence Secretary.

And it doesn't just end there, does it – for Scots in Britain are hardly shrinking violets in other fields – from Govan boy Sir Alex Ferguson in sport, managing possibly the best known football team in the world, to John Reith from Stonehaven, who built the BBC into the envy of the world. Neither they or many others like them were born with a silver spoon in their mouths to run or shape British institutions.

It is this social union that I fear for most. As the levels of bitterness and bile in the referendum debate begin to rise – as we now begin to see that the continuing UK can and will have different interests from Scots and Scotland and has every right to pursue them – – new grievances will tear us apart. What's positive about that?

Scottish nationalism – why did the tide rise?

Hugh Andrew
18 February 2014

ONE OF the most obvious yet in some ways least understood events of the past twenty years has been the resurgence of Scottish nationalism as a political force. In many ways this is rather peculiar.

Nationalism under Margaret Thatcher, always seen as the great blocking force to Scottish identity, actually did remarkably badly. Scots preferred to show their resentment through Labour. Even the crash in the SNP vote in 1979 is somewhat odd. The Scotland Bill squeaked through on a low turnout and fell to a rather dubious emendment re turnout. Yet instead of anger, Scots voters turned against the party whose rise had promoted that bill. What it actually revealed was that in the 1970s the SNP was Scotland's party of protest. Voters were reacting against Conservative and Labour and not for a new constitutional dispensation. Through the 80s and 90s the dominant political discourse was between the traditional parties in Scotland. Nationalism struggled to maintain relevance and a grip on the agenda.

It is customary to say that it was the advent of the Scottish Parliament that gave the SNP a lifeline. The fascination with how it would do in that first Holyrood election at least in part led to a status and a formalised role as the official opposition with some 36 seats in that first Parliament. The rest in some degree is history though it should not be forgotten the heavy losses the SNP suffered in the second Holyrood election. But I would like to suggest that to look simply at the advent of Holyrood as a Nationalist lifeline is facile. Something else happened in the 1990s, something that I believe gave and has given nationalists the oxygen that they needed. That something was an act of folly for which John Major's Conservative government must take responsibility but in which both Liberal Democrat and Labour parties must take their burden of guilt for failing to reverse.

What is at the root of Nationalism? What drives people to it? It is simple, it is the politics of exclusion, of alienation, of powerlessness. It is the feeling of lack of control over one's own life. Nationalism offers an easy mantra, a seductive promise that 'you' will be back in charge and not the mysterious 'them' who run your lives currently. Much as it hurts the feelings of politicians we all know that people vote far more strongly against than for, and new governments are formed less on waves of enthusiasm than of rejection of the previous. The current Nationalist surge then is less to me a statement of belief in independence than a reaction against traditional politics and politicians. So what then lies at the deep tap root of that rise?

I would argue that the real cause lies in the destruction under the name of reorganisation of local government in Scotland under the Tory gerrymander of the 90s. Let us remember that even at the time the creation of single tier authorities, their often bizarre boundaries, their wildly varying populations, were designed as a cynical manoeuvre to at least try and preserve some Tory control in local administration. The attempt failed, the legacy remains. The result is a ragbag of delegitimised authorities often not big enough to have strategic responsibility, often too small to have any real room for manoeuvre. Turnout is derisory. People don't want to stand. Their revenue-raising powers have been practically removed, their remaining powers stripped or truncated. For communities they are often irrelevant. And as a result the feeling of alienation from politics grows.

For Nationalism of course the paradox is that to feed their pretence of empowerment of the people of Scotland, to feed the alienation on which they thrive, they have to continue to undermine the institutions of civic Scotland and civic society. The tune they pretend to trumpet is diametrically opposite to the one they actually play.

Power to the people really means power to *only* those who shout power to the people.

To the opposition of all shades in Scotland this gives an opportunity. We should all speak of and strive of for the re-empowerment of local democracy, its entrenchment, a massive increase in its revenue raising power, boundaries that reflect communities and not artificial entities. We should be prepared to consider two levels of authority – at strategic and at community level. And yes, if that sounds like districts and regions so be it – if that's what people want. Instead of Holyrood's increasing centralisation we should offer true independence to the peoples and communities of Scotland.

For all of us our offer should be not the one drab grey monolithic Scotland of the Nationalist offering, but the diversity, colour, excitement and difference of the many Scotlands that exist. Geographical communities, imagined communities – it is in their enhancement that lies the true deadly threat to Nationalism and the lifeline to all who oppose it.

Scottish independence: it's all about trust

Ben Acheson
18 February 2014

POLITICS IS SHOWBIZ for the ugly. Or so they say. In reality, it is *much* more than that.

Politics is about running a country, or at least trying to get into Government in order to run a country. That is why there is one question that really matters if you are voting in Scotland's independence referendum.

Can this Scottish Government be trusted to run a country?

Providing an answer is no easy task. You could argue that the SNP has been in power since 2007 and the country has not imploded, but you could claim that total implosion is unlikely as it is propped up by the UK Government. Either way, the unprecedented nature of the debate makes judging on track records a potentially perilous endeavour.

Instead, let's look at current events and recent press coverage for indicators. It isn't unreasonable to judge a government by economic policy. For Scotland, there isn't much to say on the economy that has not been said in the past week. The currency union fiasco has been well-covered. Alex Salmond's plan was categorically torpedoed by anyone and everyone that matters in UK politics.

Even the battle-tested Nicola Sturgeon was unceremoniously mauled by Andrew Neil on the *Daily Politics Show*. It was reminiscent of the infamous Paxman-Howard interview. It was embarrassing, cringe-worthy and borderline unwatchable. It reached the point where even the most militant unionists must have started to feel a bit sorry for the normally formidable SNP Deputy Leader.

But everyone makes mistakes, even if they don't admit to them. So what else can we judge on?

Let's take the other recent media obsession; an independent Scotland's membership of the European Union. This is another topic on which the Scottish Government is unscrupulously intransigent and unbearably misguided. It argues that an independent Scotland would seamlessly transition to being an EU member state.

False.

Jose Manuel Barroso, the President of the European Commission, already quashed Alex Salmond's assertions of an inherited EU membership back in 2012. This week, he did it again. The media was whipped into a frenzy when Barroso stated that it would be 'extremely difficult, if not impossible' for an independent Scotland to obtain universal support from existing EU member states if applying to join the EU. So who do we trust? The *de facto* head of the EU or a party that has already been caught lying about the legal advice it claimed to have received on EU membership?

The astoundingly bad week for Alex Salmond and the SNP didn't end there. Adding insult to injury, the UK Energy Secretary excoriated the SNP's energy strategy in the press. He slammed its renewables vision, warning of higher bills and potential blackouts. Bear in mind that this is the same energy secretary whose support for renewables is so ardent that he is often publicly at loggerheads with other ministers in his own department. He is no 'nimbyist', sentimentalist' or 'climate denier', but even he is mystified by some of the SNP's ambitions.

As Secretary of State for Energy, Ed Davey made it clear that the shared single energy market would end with independence. He confirmed that English, Welsh and Northern Irish consumers will not continue to subsidise renewables in Scotland. He also warned that in sustained periods of low wind, an independent Scottish Government's intense focus on industrial wind turbines would mean that it could end up having to import electricity from English power stations in order to keep the lights on. This is because wind is not an uninterrupted energy source. Amongst other problems (as shown in the video below), it is inherently intermittent.

So an independent Scotland would neither have an uninterrupted source of energy nor affordable bills. Remembering that the International Energy Agency defines energy security as *'the uninterrupted availability of energy sources at an affordable price'*, does this then suggest that an independent Scotland would not be able to ensure its own energy security, something which is a key priority for any functioning Government?

Inevitably, these arguments will be dismissed as conjecture and branded as 'scaremongering'. That is always the first defence of someone who doesn't like your argument but can't provide a suitable rebuttal. However, the fact remains that the Chancellor of the Exchequer confirmed that there won't be a currency union. The President of the European Commission reaffirmed that there is no easy route into the EU. The Secretary of State for Energy warned that there will be no single energy market.

With the referendum fast approaching, there is no longer a place for 'your word versus mine' politics. Ignoring reality helps no one, not least the voters. Answers are needed. If there is a yes vote what is Plan B when there is no currency union? What are the implications when Scotland has to apply to join the EU? How will energy security be achieved when there is no shared energy market?

It is Alex Salmond, the SNP or Yes Scotland who must answer these questions. If they cannot, then can they really be trusted to run a country? The answer is a resounding 'No'.

No formal currency union! What next?

Allan Smith
20 February 2014

LAST WEEK when George Osborne delivered his speech in Edinburgh, he dealt a tremendous blow to the Yes campaign's plans for independence. Whether you agree with how he delivered his stark warning to the SNP or not, its content was a game changer. Not least because it was endorsed by the other two main political parties in the United Kingdom. I genuinely can't recall such an occurrence in my many years of following politics.

In the event of Scotland voting to separate from the United Kingdom, a formal currency union has unequivocally been ruled. More to the point, Osborne, Balls and Alexander meant it. It is simply not going to happen.

I've been struck by the shallowness of the Scottish Government's stance.

Despite its protestations that there was no "Plan B" required and a formal currency union was "inevitable" it genuinely appears as though they haven't given an alternative to a Sterling currency union a moment's thought. It has been made clear by the UK Government since this debate began that a formal currency union

191

was highly unlikely. It would have to be in the interests of the remainder of the UK.

I've always been confused by the SNP's stance on currency union in any case. If I were a supporter of independence, I would have expected to have been asked whether I wanted independence in the forthcoming referendum. What is being offered by Salmond and his government is nothing like independence.

If recent history has taught us anything, it is that monetary union without fiscal union is a broken model, and a risk to be avoided at all costs. The SNP leadership's preferred currency option (that has now been ruled out) is to suggest that an independent Scotland should take full control over its tax revenues, whilst at the same time maintaining a monetary and banking union with the remainder of the United Kingdom.

In short, its preferred option is precisely the model which has shown itself to be so prone to failure with the near collapse of the Euro. The uncertainty that is created when the stability of a monetary union is called into question can have a drastic effect on those within the currency union's economy.

A prime example of this was when the strength of the European banking system was tested during the Eurozone crisis, primarily in peripheral countries, but also in Belgium. During the crisis, bank deposits and other capital rapidly moved from financial institutions based in one set of countries, to those based in another. So in essence its preferred currency option was an incredibly risky one. This is precisely the reason why Osborne, Balls and Alexander ruled it out last week.

It has been said on a number of occasions by those advocating separation from the UK that an independent Scotland could use the pound if it liked. They're correct, Sterling's a traded currency, we could use it if we liked. However; we would have no control over our interest rates, no representation within The Treasury, no Scottish MP's to represent our monetary interests and no lender of last resort.

In short, financially in any case, we would be significantly less "independent" than we are at present. Taking the above in to account along with Salmond and Sturgeon's threats to refuse to assume liability for our portion of the UK debt and you have an economic basket case of a country.

There literally is nothing positive to say about the above option.

The logical approach would be for an independent Scotland to have its own currency. Surely that's what "independence" should mean?

The SNP has had decades to come up with a viable currency option. It's astonishing that having talked down the UK and pontificated about how Westminster politics has "held us back" for so long, it now appears to want to retain the currency that until recently according to Mr Salmond was "a millstone round our neck."

The currency aside there are numerous other significant questions relating to the economy that Salmond and his party are either unwilling or incapable of answering.

Our Financial Services sector is enormous in Scotland. Having gone through the banking crisis and replaced the failed regulator, the FSA with the newly formed FCA there has been, and continues to be significant upheaval in the industry in which I work.

The SNP can't say who would regulate our Financial Services sector in an independent Scotland.

This is, in my opinion, one of the biggest black holes in the SNP's plans for independence. To assert that there would be a smooth transition from the FCA to a new (as yet unnamed) regulator of the financial services industry in Scotland is simply not a credible stance to take. Unfortunately, this is the stance being taken by the Scottish Government. It's dangerous and it is essentially playing fast and loose with Scottish jobs and the economy.

A stark warning came from one of the biggest and most respected companies in the financial services industry earlier this week. Royal London, who own Edinburgh-based Scottish Life, warned that in the event of a Yes vote in September, they would review whether 1200 employees in Scotland could continue to service its customers across the UK. Its Chief Executive Phil Loney stated;

"It would take a lot to uproot us from Scotland. We are quite committed to it. But, if the people of Scotland did vote for independence, it becomes a foreign country, and we do what we do with any foreign markets. We look at it and decide whether it's attractive."

Now I am sure that there will be cries of "scaremonger" from those advocating independence. There always are whenever someone disagrees with Alex Salmond or questions his assertions. What Loney said, however, cannot be brushed off. Nor can Mark Carney's comments regarding currency union, nor Jose Manuel Barroso's comments regarding EU membership for an independent Scotland, nor can Osborne's speech where he ruled out a formal currency union point blank.

I have always, in truth, suspected that the SNP had a "Plan B" currency option. The fact that it appears as though it doesn't on something so fundamental to the running of a successful country merely emphasises how poorly thought out its plans for independence are.

The Financial Services industry in Scotland is looking for answers to some pretty fundamental questions. With seven months to go before the referendum, I would have expected the Scottish Government to have at least started answering them. Mind you, given the shambles its currency policy is in, perhaps I should not be too surprised that it's failing to address them.

For Scotland to be more independent people should vote No

Brian Monteith
24 February 2014

We are now at the stage of the referendum campaign where probably every weekend, and possibly midweek too, there will be a new opinion poll of some sort or other telling us about the mood swings of the Scottish people as they give greater thought to the arguments for and against Scotland leaving the united Kingdom. Some people might change their opinion when they hear something they don't like, some detail they hadn't quite appreciated, while others that are undecided could be expected to begin to take a firmer view.

As the two campaign teams, the Scottish government and the opposition parties seek to influence voters and build up a momentum in their favour they will revisit some of the issues already discussed last year in the hope that they find a silver bullet that makes their case unbeatable. One of those areas is undoubtedly going to be Scotland's future relationship with the European Union. The First Minister did himself no favours last year when he claimed to have legal opinion assuring us all that

Scotland's automatic and continuing membership of the EU was assured, but refused to release it suggesting that like all such advice it should stay confidential – only for it to be revealed later by his deputy Nicola Sturgeon that no such advice did in fact exist.

This grubby little episode was made worse when the President of the European Commission José Manuel Barosso made it explicit that Scotland would have to apply as a new member and not simply continue in membership inheriting all the treaty agreements and derogations that define the UK's current membership.

Still, for all this vital clarification no-one seriously believed that the EU would not want Scotland to become a member. The real question is what the terms of the membership would be – including the increased entry fee without Margaret Thatcher's Fontainebleau discount and the EU treaty clauses that UK governments of all hues have previously worked hard to reject – now being thrust upon us that could result in us having border controls or different more costly employment conditions.

When pressed in an interview recently, President Barosso went further and explained that Scotland's membership might be difficult or even impossible if some members states did not agree to the terms, citing the example of Kosovo's membership being vetoed not just by Spain but also Cyprus, Greece, Romania and Slovakia.

I believe the position of Barosso was not bluster or scaremongering but a robust attempt to mark out the realities of how difficult the EU negotiations will be – he was dampening the over-optimistic expectations raised by Alex Salmond who has an interest in suggesting membership will be seamless. Scottish EU membership will come at a price – like all memberships. It's not a new position by the way, his predecessor Romano Prodi said the same, and the Council President, Van Rompuy, has now backed Barroso up. Even the former EU Commission Director General

Jim Currie who favours Scotland's EU membership has said "it would involve inevitable negations that would be rather tough".

We can be certain then that an independent Scotland will apply for EU membership – and to ensure it gets in and there are no vetoes – has to concede generous terms. By definition this means that Scotland's membership will be *more costly* and *more restrictive* than that of the UK with its various derogations, discounts and treaty exclusions.

One such example surfaced at the weekend when Donato Raponi, head of the EC taxation department, explained that once an accession treaty is agreed it is "no longer possible for a member state to introduce special VAT rates. The member state must apply the EU rules." The UK enjoys zero per cent VAT on 54 areas because of a longstanding agreement, an agreement that will fall once Scotland breaks away from the UK. The chances of winning back those terms must be slim, if they exist at all, affecting the cost of books, equipment for the disabled, children's clothes, shipbuilding and aircraft repair.

Now let's also accept that Salmond is right and that the UK in the end concedes a currency union, however, it too will still come at a price. Never mind the price laid out by Osborne, Balls and Alexander – Governor Carney laid out the technical requirements that include the ceding of sovereignty to the Bank of England, the UK Treasury and Westminster – and, tellingly, the nationalists have not challenged these assertions.

We therefore arrive at the strong possibility that is entirely plausible – that an independent Scotland will be under greater control and scrutiny from the EU and Westminster than it is now, incurring greater costs, while having less clout – than if Scotland stayed in the UK under existing arrangements. That's without evening considering the further devolution that comes after the Scotland Act 2012 kicks-in during 2015/16 and if further fiscal powers are devolved.

Irrespective of how Scots feel about the current terms of EU membership, we also know from opinion polling that a majority of two to one want a referendum on EU membership – but that it has been ruled out by the SNP if Scotland votes for independence – even on the new (far poorer) terms Salmond and Sturgeon will have to negotiate.

Now if that is not enough to make those thinking of voting Yes think again then consider this scenario.

An independent Scotland negotiates its membership of the EU (undoubtedly on poorer terms than currently exist) but refuses to grant the Scottish people a say in EU membership. Meanwhile the UK moves to having its own referendum on its "improved terms" negotiated by Cameron (or even Miliband who may yet adopt this approach) and these are accepted by the British people. Thus Scotland would have even worse membership terms than the rest of the UK – it would be even less 'independent' than the UK viz a viz the European Union.

Or, after the UK EU referendum, the new terms are rejected and the UK leaves the EU – achieving complete sovereign independence.

In either scenario, whether in or out of the EU, the UK will have let its people decide and be more "independent" of the EU than Scotland *while still continuing to oversee Scotland's finances.*

The conclusion is simple, if ironic. To gain the greatest degree of independence for Scotland, whether inside or outside the EU, people should vote No. Such is the SNP's version of independence.

The truth is out there – but don't expect to find it in politics

James Corbett
25 February 2014

I'VE JUST FINISHED a short online course on forensic science and as I went through the material I was struck by how easy it can be to take a piece of evidence and reach the wrong conclusion because of personal prejudices. Twisting the evidence to suit a theory or considering the evidence to be more conclusive than it really is.

A foreign hair on a body gives you a DNA match to someone with a criminal record. Your first instinct is to make this person your prime suspect, but who's to say that the hair wasn't transferred from the passenger seat of a taxi at some point earlier in the day? As the case of Shirley McKie demonstrated, fingerprint analysis isn't always an exact science. Visual comparison by trained technicians is a key part of the process and, as we all know, people can make mistakes.

In the same way investigators rely on forensic science to provide greater levels of information to help them catch criminals, the public are relying on both sides of the referendum debate to provide information to help them decide how to vote.

There's a near constant demand from the pubic for "facts" about the independence referendum. They want guarantees about what will happen if however Scotland votes; whether it's a definitive answer on currency arrangements, or the possibility of more powers within the UK. As far as I can tell the only certainty either side can truly offer is that nothing is certain.

Some answers are more likely to be accurate than others. Sometimes there's historical evidence that can be used to demonstrate a trend or the past experience of a foreign country can be used as an (arguable) comparison. Whatever the case, it's almost impossible for Better Together or Yes Scotland to answer the public's questions with absolute certainty, despite suggestions to the contrary.

In some ways the two campaigns are dealing with the opposite ends of the same problem. Many of the Yes campaign's arguments have been reduced to a level so childishly simplistic, to try to connect with voters, that their proposition is in danger of no longer reflecting the likely realities of independence. Saying that the opinion of the rUK on a currency union would change after a Yes vote amounts to saying "trust me, I'm a politician."

I'm sure at some point someone will ask the obvious question and inquire whether this possibility of positions changing after a Yes vote extends to the contents of the White Paper.

Meanwhile Better Together is still trying to find a way to make the complex, but important, details of the UK's benefits to Scotland accessible and memorable to voters. Yes, there's certainly an advantage in having the Bank of England as a lender of last resort, but how many people can honestly say they understand what a lender of last resort does?

The independence referendum is still more than six months away, but no-one should expect that all the questions being asked of both sides will be answered by the 18th of September. In fact many of the questions being asked are the same ones we've been asking of politicians at every election for as long as we've lived in a democracy. What will the tax rates be? What ideas do you have for the economy?

Both sides can try to predict the future, but neither side can promise to deliver it. There's already an enormous amount of available information about both independence and staying in the UK. How people vote is often as much about gut instinct as detailed analysis of political manifestos. You can give the public more than enough information to make the decision with their eyes wide open, but you can't avoid the fact that many, if not most, people will continue to see that information through a lens tinted by their own political beliefs.

Although people will often demand more information, if the information they're given doesn't suit their underlying beliefs then it's often quickly dismissed as wrong. In politics, the credibility of an information source can be more important than the content of the information. If you believe the source, you believe the information. In a debate that often boils down to "my expert is better than your expert" credibility has never been more vital.

People are more engaged in Scottish politics and there's more information to engage with than ever before. The risk is that people are attributing too much certainty to the answers politicians give them. In politics many questions don't have a simple right or wrong answer. Usually there are several answers and it's up to the public to decide which answer they trust most and hope they aren't disappointed.

As Churchill said; "Politics is the ability to foretell what is going to happen tomorrow, next week, next month and next year. And to have the ability afterwards to explain why it didn't happen."

Follow James on Twitter @jtrcorbett

Paul Krugman – bluff or bluster?

Bill Jamieson
26 February 2014

IT IS NOT OFTEN – indeed, it would be about as frequent as a blue moon, when a Conservative chancellor could cite with favour an opinion of the American economist Paul Krugman. But with First Minister Alex Salmond's admission of 'Plan B' on Scotland's currency plans on independence, blue moons are now upon us.

The SNP leadership has let it be known that it intends to retain the pound as Scotland's national currency in the event of independence, even though a full currency union as envisaged in its White Paper would be denied to it. The proposal – similar to the currency arrangements for Ecuador which continues to use the US dollar – would result in an independent Scotland continuing to use sterling but with no say in monetary policy, the setting of interest rates and, crucially, without the Bank of England acting as a lender of last resort to the country's banking institutions.

Enter left (and notably Left) Professor Krugman, scourge of the Westminster coalition's "austerity" policies who has continually argued for higher government spending – and

203

borrowing – as the sure means to recover from the post financial crisis recession.

This uber-Keynesian critique was frequently echoed by the Left-of-Centre SNP administration which has constantly urged the Westminster government to embark on ambitious public spending and infrastructure projects (so much, it seems, for its constant hectoring to create a Norway-style long-term oil fund: few parties have more championed ever-greater public spending than the SNP – and to hell with borrowing, debt and 'long term insurance funds').

As matters have turned out, the UK economy is now enjoying a much wider recovery than most experts had predicted – although it could hardly be said that the slowdown in the rate of growth in government spending could be compared to the period of immediate post-war austerity.

Now, in an article for the *New York Times*, Krugman has waded into the controversy over the SNP's fall-back currency plans. "Independence", he writes, "would have to rest on a sound monetary foundation. And the independence movement has me worried, because what it has said on that that crucial subject seems deeply muddle-headed."

"What the independence movement says is that there's no problem – Scotland will simply stay on the pound. That is, however, much more problematic than they seem to realize."

The rest of the UK, of course, would not be able to prevent the Scots from using the pound any more than the United States can't stop Ecuador from using dollars. "But the lesson of the Euro crisis, surely, is that sharing a common currency without having a shared federal government is very dangerous."

Indeed, he warns, a 'currency tag-along' Scotland "would be in even worse shape than the Euro countries, because the Bank of England would be under no obligation to act as lender of last resort to Scottish banks – that is, it would arguably take even less responsibility for local financial stability than the pre-Draghi

ECB. And it would fall very far short of the post-Draghi ECB, which has in effect taken on the role of lender of last resort to Euro zone governments, too."

What would happen, he goes on to ask, if something goes wrong, if there's a slump in Scotland's economy? "As part of the United Kingdom, Scotland would receive large de facto aid, just like a US state (or Wales); if it were on its own, it would be on its own, like Portugal."

"Now, Scotland would presumably have high labour mobility – assuming it manages somehow to join the EU … it would be under the Single European Act, and it sort of shares a common language with England.'

"But that's not necessarily a good thing: what we're seeing in places like Portugal is large-scale emigration of young workers, leaving a diminished population to bear the fiscal burden of caring for the elderly.

Again, I can understand Scots grievances. But if they really want to do this, they had better get real about money."

Such is the Krugman verdict on the SNP's currency tag-along option for the SNP. The alternative 'Plan B' would be setting up a separate Scottish currency, and that would be deeply prejudicial for Scotland's business community.

Already, George Osborne and Chief Treasury Secretary Danny Alexander have attacked the proposal as a "second best" option for Scots…. "Our question to the nationalists – are you really saying second best is good enough for Scotland?" And former Labour chancellor Alistair Darling, leading the 'Better Together' anti-independence campaign, echoed the government's criticism this week, saying it would leave Scotland in a financial "straitjacket".

Such bold sentiments are barely worth the breath expended on them as they would immediately be denounced by the 'Yes' campaign as yet more negativity and "scare-mongering" or "all bluff and bluster".

But given Krugman's status as a poster child for SNP economic commentators, this critique may be harder to deploy. The SNP stance for now is that whoever will be the government of the rUK, in 2015-16 it will buckle and come to sing Alex Salmond's tune. It is not logic that is being deployed, or any rational argument, but blind faith that this gamble will work and, if it doesn't, then 'tag-along Plan B' is a credible basis for an "independent" (sic) Scotland. When the Krugman guru now pronounces this as dangerous, who am I to argue?

Why break something that can instead be improved?

Robert Kilgour
26 February 2014

I AM OFTEN asked what I think about independence and how it will affect business. Firstly let me give some context.

I am a simple, hard working Scottish businessman who is endeavouring to continue to attract investment into Scotland and to create jobs in the same way that I have been doing for the last thirty-plus years with some reasonable success.

I am what might be called a serial entrepreneur, investor and property developer.

I was the original founder of Four Seasons Health Care which is now the UK's largest care home operator with over 500 homes and over 30,000 staff. In 1990 I founded Dow Investments Plc (for general investments) and in 2004 the Renaissance Care Group (a Scottish care home operator) which currently has twelve care homes and around 750 staff throughout Scotland. I am also a co-founder and Director of NW Systems Group (IP video and security) and of Kingdom FM Radio – the local radio franchise holder for Fife.

In addition I have spent over twenty years actively fundraising for Macmillan Cancer Support and have raised close to £2m over this time, mainly to fund projects in Scotland.

My late Father used to urge me to work hard, play hard and always put something back and I have done my best to follow this good advice during all of my adult life.

I am a very proud and passionate Scot and I am also a very proud citizen of the UK. I believe firmly that the UK's diversity is its greatest strength – not its greatest weakness.

I accept that Scotland could survive as an independent country and I certainly would not leave the country if it did become independent but I firmly believe that a 'Yes' vote and the independence that would follow would simply not be in the best interests of Scotland or the Scottish people.

I also firmly believe that Governments don't create jobs – their role is to create the right climate for those of us in business to create the jobs that will then supply them with the much needed taxes that enable Governments to then choose how to allocate these collected funds across all of the essential public services that they are responsible for delivering.

I really feel, and in fact I have already found recently, that the threat of independence is a direct negative barrier to attracting investment and jobs into Scotland.

I always saw, and still see, Devolution as an ever-evolving process and this is evidenced by all of the additional powers shortly to come in from the Scotland Act 2012 – and I am further strongly in favour of more fiscal powers being devolved to the Scottish Parliament in the very near future.

However, and this is the question I always come back to – why break up something that is currently being improved and can be improved still further?

Standard Life's Plan B trumps Salmond's case for independence

Brian Monteith
28 February 2014

If you thought the visits to Edinburgh of Governor Carney and George Osborne were nothing other than mere obtuse technicalities or Tory bluff and bluster then fair enough, that's your right. You may just shrug your shoulders and say, "hell mend them, who are they to tell us what to do."

And indeed, who are they, a mere Canadian and and Englishman, what right have they to tell us what currency a free independent Scotland can use? If they place limitations on us having a formal agreement on using the pound then we can just use it anyway without their agreement. Like Panama or Ecuador uses the dollar.

Well, Standard Life has now spoken and it is an Edinburgh company. A very successful one. It's not foreign, not from the home counties or the dreaded City of London – it's as Scottish as Edinburgh Rock. It has been so successful that it has built up a huge business selling pensions, savings and other financial products – to English people. Some ninety per cent of its business is outside Scotland and mostly in England. So, for it, issues of which currency to use, what regulations to work under are very, very important and can be quantified and considered in a non-political, non-partisan and objective way.

Standard Life can say what it wants without any intention to bully, without any agenda to bluster and it cannot afford to be bluffing. Standard Life is not telling anyone how to vote and has made that clear; it is simply respecting its shareholders, customers and employees in that it has a fiduciary duty to report what it sees as the risks to its operations and therefore its profits (and thus its dividends), its investment growth (and therefore its customers pensions and savings) and its future competitiveness and sustainability (which is what underpins the thousands of jobs it provides).

It has to be honest and frank about these things now or face legal actions from those stakeholders in the future – just as RBS faces legal action for what it did or didn't say before its rights issue related to the cataclysmic ABN-Amro takeover.

Let's get this straight; there will be no formal currency union, it is not in the UK's interest to have one. Period. Some people have said that the currency issue is too high falutin to matter – but it goes to the heart of what an independent country is about. *Being independent.*

Carney came to Edinburgh and told us the technical methods for sharing any currency would require the mutual sharing of sovereignty or it would not work. Osborne came to Edinburgh and told us that those technicalities would involve a ceding of English sovereignty that his permanent secretary could not recommend and that he could not accept. Labour and the Lib Dems agreed.

Now, in the absence of that shared pound being available Standard Life is saying that – as a British company – it would have to relocate much of its operations to, where else, but somewhere in Britain. Using the pound without Carney's central bank and having different regulations is too risky for its business – it will lose customers that will want guarantees of security.

The implications of all of this go beyond Standard Life; now that it has had the courage to speak out others will do so too. The idea that RBS will stay headquartered in Scotland is difficult to square-off. The revival of the Nat West brand that it bought, with an HQ in London is far more likely. It is, after all, owned 83 per cent by the UK which means 72 per cent is owned by England, Wales and Northern Ireland taxpayers. All the commercial issues that affect Standard Life (regulation, customer base, oversight of governance, currency) affect RBS – and TSB, Lloyds (BoS & Scottish Widows) and many others as well.

Take them out, or even just reduce them in scale of operations, and Edinburgh changes away from being a financial centre with a highly attractive balance between private and public sector employment – and all the spending that comes from the former – towards being a government, legal and education centre funded out of the public purse. Look for big shops shutting, private schools closing and investment finding more attractive locations (Leeds and Manchester). Scotland's economic growth will be concentrated in Aberdeen (so long as the oil lasts).

We owe Standard Life a debt of gratitude for telling it as it sees it. We can still vote for independence if we judge it worth the risk – but at least we now know some of the cost to the Edinburgh and Scottish economy in earnings, spending on local services and jobs.

Edinburgh will become a museum piece – a nice museum piece – but little more than a testimony to the good times of the union after the enlightenment. Edinburgh used to be the world capital of publishing – not any more it's not. It used to be an international centre for brewing – not any more it's not.

It is still a highly attractive financial centre – but after independence of the type Alex Salmond is selling it faces mass emigration of its business base.

Will the last fund manager please switch off the lights.

"Wait and see" approach leaves Yes campaign without credibility

Allan Smith
4 March 2014

STANDARD LIFE'S announcement last week that it "may" move its operations from Edinburgh down to England was met with such vitriol by the pro-separation movement that its position is beginning to look quite absurd.

Within minutes of Standard Life detailing that in the event of a Yes vote, carrying on its business in Scotland using its current model may be untenable. The Yes campaign's "cybernats" began attacking the company left, right and centre online. Threats to "close accounts" "switch pension providers" etc were everywhere on Twitter and Facebook as the yes campaign's online keyboard warriors began their collective gnashing of teeth.

In truth what Standard Life, which has 4 million UK based customers (ninety per cent south of the border) and employs 5,000 people in Scotland said last week, could not have really been any clearer. Gerry Grimstone, the firm's chairman, said:

213

"We have been based in Scotland for 189 years and we are very proud of our heritage. Scotland has been a good place from which to run our business and to compete around the world.

"We very much hope that this can continue. But if anything were to threaten this, we will take whatever action we consider necessary – including transferring parts of our operations from Scotland – in order to ensure continuity and to protect the interests of our stakeholders."

In addition the chief executive, David Nish, said the company had started to register companies in England, but did not say where Standard Life's new headquarters could be.

One of the main concerns expressed by Standard Life in its annual report was the credibility of the Scottish Government's commitment for an independent Scotland to join the European Union by the preferred March 2016 target date proposed in its White Paper. Essentially the only people who appear to believe that this timescale is achievable are those within the SNP.

The financial services firm, which has £237bn under management, highlighted uncertainties over an independent Scotland's currency, the shape of its monetary system, regulation of financial services and taxes. Given that the Scottish Government is unwilling to clarify what currency we would be using post separation or indeed mention who would be regulating our Financial Services industry after September the 18th, it's hardly surprising to me as a Financial Adviser that Standard Life appears to be as concerned as it is.

By contrast, and quite telling, has been the Yes camp's response to Standard Life's announcement. During a telephone debate on BBC Radio 5Live last week, Michelle Thomson, the Managing Director of Business for Scotland (the yes camp's business group), told me that;

"what Standard Life are saying now isn't what they would be saying after independence."

Now wait a minute; where have I heard that before? Isn't that what the Yes camp saying on a currency union post-independence? Or indeed the regulation of our Financial Services sector post-independence? Or finally Scotland's status within the EU?

In other words; they will all assert that everything will be absolutely fine, but they don't really know for sure, *you'll just have to trust them.*

It wasn't just Standard Life which expressed concern about the uncertainty in the business world caused by the Scottish Government's inability to come up with a credible "Plan B" on currency and other areas. Take RBS, buried deep within the largely state-owned Edinburgh-based bank's annual report there was a frank assessment of the consequences of a "yes vote". The bank said that the Scottish Independence referendum was a risk to its business and had already "negatively affected" its business. It stated:

"The group's businesses, earnings and financial condition have been and will continue to be negatively affected by global economic conditions, the instability in the global financial markets and increased competition and political risks including proposed referenda on Scottish independence and UK membership of the EU.

"Together with a perceived increased risk of default on the sovereign debt of certain European countries and unprecedented stresses on the financial system within the eurozone, these factors have resulted in significant changes in market conditions including interest rates, foreign exchange rates, credit spreads, and other market factors and consequent changes in asset valuations."

RBS also warns on page 206 of the document that that it relied heavily on the UK government's credit rating, which could be impacted by independence.

"Furthermore, the group's borrowing costs and its access to the debt capital markets and other sources of liquidity depend

significantly on its and the UK government's credit ratings which would be likely to be negatively impacted by political events, such as an affirmative outcome of the referendum for the independence of Scotland."

Now it's clear that neither Standard Life, RBS nor Scottish Life – who last week stated that in the unlikely event of a Yes vote in September Scotland would be treated as a *"foreign country"* – are definitely saying they would leave Scotland. The concerns that they have raised, however, can no longer be dismissed by the Yes camp with claims of "scaremongering" or being "Tory-led" or "anti-Scottish". The stakes are too high for this sort of nonsense.

By stating "everything will be all right on the night" the SNP and the yes camp are playing fast and loose with Scottish jobs.

As an Independent Financial Adviser I have in the past placed business with Standard Life, Scottish Life and RBS and shall continue to do so. However, given the upheaval in my industry and the fact that the FCA is only now beginning to get a handle on its role as regulator of the UK's financial services industry, the stance being taken by the Scottish Government is as dangerous as it is foolish.

Scotland has a proud history in banking and financial services although the actions of some have caused this to be significantly damaged since 2008. Just as we seem to be getting over the worst of the financial crisis the Yes campaign seems keen to add another new level of uncertainty to the industry and in doing so is risking Scottish jobs in the process.

A clear plan for regulation of an independent Scotland's financial services sector is absolutely essential if the Yes campaign is to regain any credibility whatsoever in this area.

Wait and see can never be the preferred option. It is simply not a credible plan for the future of Scotland's financial services industry.

Behind the mask of "uncertainty" resides a real fear of independence

Bill Jamieson
12 March 2014

SIX MONTHS of the independence battle still to go, the artillery smoke is growing and in the hall apprehensive viewers search for the doors marked 'Exit'. Chief among them so far is Standard Life. Now comes the iconic Alliance Investment Trust with its huge retail investor following and overall more than £10 billion of savings under management.

It announced last week it has set up two new subsidiaries in England to prepare for the possibility of an independent Scotland.

Am I surprised? No. As I have pointed out here before, if these companies did not respond to the growing "uncertainty" over the future taxation and regulation of savings in Scotland, their customers would certainly take matters into their own hands and move.

But what has taken me aback is the insouciance so far displayed by independence campaigners and their sympathisers in the Scottish commentariat. The fears, they say, are overblown. Or it's all George Osborne's fault for not agreeing to currency sharing. Or it's just more 'Project Fear'. Others have affected not to notice, or feel it's too minor a matter on which to comment.

Yet here is one of the biggest and most historic institutions in Scottish financial services. Indeed, if you had to name a single financial institution that best encapsulates Scotland's distinctive presence in the investment world, this 126 year-old institution based in Dundee could lay fair claim. It has stood aloof from the day-trading frenzy of London. It is conservative in style and approach. And it prides itself in its separateness and independence.

It also has millions of customers. Its fund selection platform Alliance Trust Savings on its £5.4 billion of assets under management. Chief executive Katherine Garrett-Cox, says the move has been undertaken to meet customer concerns over the future taxation of savings and pension plans should Scotland opt to leave the union.

She said it is "critical" that the company is able to ensure continuity and protection for customers – around 80 per cent of whom live outside Scotland. The trust estimates that about two thirds of its shareholders are also based outwith Scotland. She went on to say that this did not signal a wholesale shift of the company's domicile outwith Scotland – but notably added the words "at this point".

There are also tens of thousands of Scots who invest through the Alliance Trust Savings fund platform, equally concerned about the future treatment of savings built up out of already taxed earned income.

It is the muted response of the Yes campaign – and more often an apparent indifference – that in my view gives the game away. It is revealing of a mind-set that struggles to imagine what the problem is and why this should matter. The need to retain and expand a large and successful component of Scotland's economy is of lesser import than victory in the campaign to tax and spend in the manner they would like.

The SNP is, after all, a Left of Centre party. It has made no secret of this. It favours high public spending and a large government share in GDP. It believes economic growth comes through public spending. And it has championed the extension of "free" public services and benefits – retail politics of the most blatant sort.

Companies like Alliance Trust carefully word their statements to make clear two things: first, that they are not expressing a corporate view one way or another on independence; and second that they are responding to "uncertainty".

Doubtless this is why a growing number of large companies – BP, Aggreko, Lloyds Banking Group, now Standard Life and Alliance – have responded in the way they have.

But there is a growing apprehension behind the masking word of "uncertainty" over the Leftward lurch that an independent Scotland would be likely to undertake. There is little by way of a forceful Conservative opposition to speak of. A Left leaning SNP, together with Labour fellow-travellers intent on pursuing their atavistic class war, levelling income inequality, making the 'fat cats' pay more and generally purging Scotland of reactionary and politically resistant wealthy elements – would have untrammelled reign.

In this environment – a Scotland governed not by a "nationalist" party but a sectarian class war party – it is not inconceivable that the targets and their capital would move. Turkeys, after all, don't queue peacefully at the door of the slaughterhouse.

There is another likelihood. With the forecast fall in North Sea oil tax revenues, future Scottish administrations would be pressured to find extra tax revenues from elsewhere rather than cut public spending for those constituencies on which they are critically dependent for votes. Those who have savings and investments in Scottish institutions – particularly as some 80 per cent or more of them are not domiciled in Scotland and thus do not have a vote – would be highly attractive and easily pick-able low-hanging fruit for a Left-leaning nationalist Scotland.

Paranoia? It is not the rabid Right wing London establishment that has raised the spectre of an independent Scotland failing to honour its share of UK public debt. It is Scotland's First Minister. And nor should we regard this as some temporary, passing threat. It would not surprise at all if Scotland's share of that debt becomes the target of a sustained 'Can't Pay, Won't Pay' campaign that could dominate an independent Scotland for years.

Alliance Trust has acted to defend the interests of millions of its customers. Expect others in the sector to follow suit. It's not "uncertainty" these customers fear as much as their likely fate in the cull that lies beyond.

SNP childcare costings shown as pure fantasy

Neil Craig
13 March 2014

THE BIG money promise the SNP made in its White Paper was that if the Scots voted for separation the SNP would immediately provide:

• Thirty hours of childcare per week in term time for all three and four-year-olds, as well as vulnerable two-year-olds.

As I mentioned in a previous ThinkScotland article this means 150,000 kids or 200,000 hours so at least another £1 billion in extra taxes. That's 3p on income tax or equivalent the SNP is promising.

This promise was always something like the "bedroom tax" – which the SNP already had the power legislate over if it thought doing something more desirable than using the issue as a totem, which obviously requires not doing anything because if it fixed the problem it couldn't denounce it).

As a promise it is very carefully targeted. Child carer costs are a dreadful additional expense for parents of young children and a serious disincentive to those who don't yet have them. The promise to wave them away with a little economic magic if only people vote for separation was likely to be greeted with relief by a particularly desperate demographic group. Which is, of course, why the SNP, so cynically, made the promise.

The particular economic magic it promised was that its figures showed that if the state simply took on the job of paying for child carer costs it promised enough mothers would join the workforce to bring in matching extra taxes to pay for it all. But only with independence – because otherwise the extra tax money would go to Westminster, and Westminster, being the wicked uncles the SNP say, would never consent to return any of it (even though under the Barnett formula the wicked uncles have always given Alex more per capita than they reserve for the English).

The logic all depends on the SNP being able to say, with certainty, that the tax rise would match the cost rise. Fortunately for the SNP, as we have repeatedly seen, it has no difficulty saying, with certainty, things which simply aren't true.

Scottishpol, the personal blog of the *Sunday Herald* political editor Tom Gordon takes up the story.

"I've received a response to a Freedom of Information request I submitted to the Scottish Government asking for "the full results of any modelling which has been done" on the specific childcare proposals in the White Paper.

It turns out the Scottish Government didn't do ANY modelling of its own flagship policy.

It modelled the impact of more women in the workforce... "rather than directly modelling the impact of improved childcare itself".

To be fair, better childcare *might* bring lots more women into the workforce, and *might* raise lots more tax, but to advance a totemic policy on the basis of crossed fingers rather than rigorous analysis – and to give the impression it would be self-funding – seems pretty extraordinary to me.

If that's the standard for White Paper policies, folk may wonder what else is wishful thinking."

So the SNP made it up. Its "estimate" of the extra money just came out of thin air.

It is actually worse than that because the current cost of child carers is not something set in stone about which the SNP can do nothing. It is the direct and deliberate cost of government policy.

Here is a list of childcare costs around the OECD countries, calibrated in terms of average wages which I think is a good comparison because, with little technology required, that really should be what makes up childcare costs.

SOURCE: OECD

Switzerland 77.7
UK 40.9
Ireland 45.2
USA 38.1
New Zealand 28.6
Canada 29.5
Japan 28.1
Australia 22.5
Slovenia 19.9
OECD, all 18.
Austria 16.8
Germany 14.1
Israel 18.3
Norway 10.8
France 16.5
Netherlands 13.2
Denmark 11.2
Korea 8.5
Finland 12.2
Czech Republic 10.6
Luxembourg 8.7
Iceland 7.9

Portugal 7.7
Poland 7.1
Spain 8.2
Belgium 5.8
Sweden 7.1
Hungary 6.2
Slovak Republic 7.4
Estonia 6.6
Greece 4.9

That is what I call a wide disparity. Note that Sweden, Belgium, Iceland, Luxembourg and Finland are all countries as wealthy as us or slightly more and all countries with good welfare systems so it is not credible that they are keeping costs down by dropping standards – even if the state were not to notice the parents would.

Note also that all of the least expensive 13 except Iceland are EU members so, for once, the EU regulatory regime cannot be to blame.

The basic rule here is that if something is being done abroad at a certain price it is possible to do it at that price here, and if it isn't being done cheaper here it must, other things being equal, be that our government is more restrictive than abroad's. This applies with costs of nuclear plants, housing, building projects, tunnelling. It must also apply to childcare.

The cost of the last 13 averages 7.7% of average income. With Britain at 40.9%, that must mean the level of state parasitism is 81% of the total cost.

Obviously not only is this cruel to parents it produces a strong discouragement to the birth of children, particularly among the middle class, who are neither rich enough to afford it, nor poor enough to be due it for free. It is difficult to think of something more likely to, over generations, destroy our nation. And keeping a significant proportion of parents out of the workforce has major economic effects.

Note that Estonia, with virtually the lowest costs (6.6%), is also a deeply libertarian state (largely because after decades of Soviet rule the people are unimpressed with the promises of statists). I do not seek separation from the rest of Britain but if we were to be governed by politicians like Estonia's I would not fear the outcome. Unfortunately it is difficult to conceive of politicians less akin to the entrepreneurial, libertarian free market Estonians than the current Holyrood Numptocracy.

How to solve it:

Rather than spend a lot of time fighting over each regulation and slowly hacking away at the bureaucracy, why not simply introduce a new class of child care? Say that anybody is allowed to set up as a "Childminder" (as opposed to Child carer) so long as all their advertising includes "not government regulated" and that such childminders are allowed to include any sort of liability waiver. I assume liability law is why the US costs are almost as high as Britain's. Any parents are free to choose.

Current law on everybody includes the need for public liability insurance and that would remain and might well become the basis of a free market, just as France avoids most of our housing regulation by requiring builder's insurance on all new housing.

Note also that in Scotland, almost all regulatory powers are held by Holyrood. Thus this reform could be carried out here without any interference from either Westminster or Brussels.

Be it Devo Marx or Devo Max, the Scottish people should decide

James Corbett
25 March 2014

ALTHOUGH we're only at the halfway stage in the Scottish party conference season, we've reached a significant milestone in the independence debate. Yes, yes, there have been quite a lot of milestones already; a year to go, 200 days to go, six months to go, etc, but this one isn't so much about the timing as it is the proposition. We can now definitively say, that if there's a No vote, the Scottish Parliament will be given further powers beyond what was set out in the Scotland Act 2012.

For the Liberal Democrats this is nothing new, they've been proud federalists for decades. The Scottish Conservatives may not have presented the details of their proposition yet, but based on the Prime Minister's conference speech and public comments by other senior figures it's safe to say they'll back Scotland having some degree of further control over taxation at the very least. Scottish Labour's proposals may be overtly political and designed to appeal more to the party faithful than the wider public, more DevoMarx than DevoMax, but they do demonstrate a willingness to go beyond the powers devolved as a result of the Calman Commission.

So why then does an ICM poll published in this week's *Scotland on Sunday* suggest that less than 40% of voters believe that in the event of a No vote Scotland will receive further powers?

Nationalists will suggest that this is evidence that the people of Scotland will not be fooled by promises of "jam tomorrow', a phrase I have come to loathe. Arguably if supporters of the UK are promising jam tomorrow then so are the nationalists. Their promises that a vote for independence guarantees a brighter future for Scotland isn't so much jam tomorrow as jam everyday, as long as you vote Yes.

The biggest difficulty in crafting a single devolution plan is that it's a bit like showing someone a piece of string and asking how many different ways there are to cut it up. The number of possible alternative answers is huge and different people are going to have different ideas of what's best. Independence on the other hand is a more easily defined concept; all the power in Scotland (assuming you ignore the powers handed over to the EU, as so many nationalists seem to).

What the Labour plan has demonstrated quite clearly though, is that the shape of any further devolution shouldn't be decided on the back of an election result or driven by the ideology of a single party. Nationalists have incessantly demanded the pro-UK parties lay out their plans for further devolution. Unlike the SNP's White Paper, which has been adopted wholesale by Yes Scotland, Better Together isn't going to be able to hold up a single, unified, vision of Scotland's future after a No vote.

The parties in Better Together have such different visions of that future that getting them to agree some kind of formal "Calman 2.0" blueprint before the referendum would be both difficult and a distraction from the central question of independence. Although once the Scottish Conservatives publish the results of the Strathclyde Commission I imagine the first Venn diagrams showing where the various plans overlap will appear in a matter of hours.

If the Conservatives, Labour and the Liberal Democrats really want to demonstrate a willingness to get Scotland the right powers for the future then the best option is pledge the creation of an independent devolution commission after a No vote. If left to individual parties to determine what the next tranche of powers will be, it's far more likely to be for powers that suit only their own political beliefs. Scottish Labour's devolution proposal demonstrates that no plan for devolution cooked up by a single party is going to be agreeable to the majority of voters.

Devolution may come at the hands of one party or another but the thinking behind the proposal has always been from a mixture of sources. The work of the Scottish Constitutional Convention contributed heavily to the settlement that created the Scottish Parliament and the Calman Commission was the foundation of the Scotland Act 2012.

A devolution settlement that voters of all sides can believe in will only come from a proposal that's backed by a range of voices, both political and civic, after a careful and mature discussion. Rather than seeing any one of the pro-UK parties proposals as a blueprint for the next stage in devolution, think of them as a demonstration of willingness to engage and participate in the wider discussion.

The three pro-UK parties might not be able to present a united front when it comes to what powers they'd like to see devolved but I suspect they will unite behind a pledge to support some kind of new constitutional convention. The decision on whether Scotland should be independent isn't being left to the politicians to decide, nor should the blueprint of future devolution.

The White Paper's Black Hole

Peter Smaill
31 March 2014

A BILLION HERE, a billion there....

...and soon you are talking real money. Thus went the (misattributed) quote of American senator, Everett Dirksen, some fifty years ago. It is, however, a phrase of *current* resonance; for in the debate about Scottish independence, for all its surface economic plausibility, the numbers hidden from public view are, on any analysis, very real money indeed.

The nationalist cause should like Dirksen, who elsewhere declaimed "Stronger than all the armies, is an idea whose time has come." Fifty years on, that idea is still equality of opportunity in government, education and society. On such a view, the seemingly unexpected drop in attributable oil revenues to pay for equality measures – from c.£8bn annually to £5bn – is just a blip: and, ignoring the poor record of recent finds, accellerating decommissioning costs and the impact of shale oil on global energy prices, the case for independence may be emotionally unstoppable.

On the calculating side of the brain, the oil will pay for everything. But will it?

That's the £3bn adverse swing on the *income side*. On the liabilities list, the discourse is much more serious, and that's not because of asset falls: Scotland has huge, unseen, off balance sheet ("OBS") liabilities which, not suprisingly, were scarcely mentioned in the 730 pages of the White Paper. Like the Titanic's iceberg, the majority of the bulk of public indebtedness is invisible from the bridge and the remainder often shrouded in accounting fog. But the peril is real.

The very real money is unfunded state sector pensions. In the UK as a whole these stand at £919 billion, and are off balance sheet. The Scottish Public Pensions Authority has fessed up to £60bn of these submerged debts, but as Scotland has 8.3 per cent of UK population and, illustratively, 9 per cent of NHS employees, the true figure of OBS is likely to reach over £80bn. In nearly all departments, due to topography and the public sector culture, Scotland has more State workers per capita than the rest of the UK and thus just a one per cent differential (say a general 9.3 per cent share) across the board would imply £9 bn of excess liability, helping make Scottish money market credit more expensive.

As recently been apparent, compliance across the board with EU requirements for full solvency of final salary pension schemes may cost firms as much as £225bn. Then there are our state sector employees, such as our principal civil servants, who benefit from a generous range of options: "classic, premium, classic plus and "nuvos" schemes": liability unquantified. As the SPPA, the statutory body appointed to run public sector schemes to the highest standards of governance says of its own scheme: " The Scottish Public Pensions Agency is unable to identify its share of the underlying assets and liabilities." *Quis custodiet ipsos custodies?* could be its motto, or better, epitaph: who will be the custodian of the custodian?

How, then, can the Scottish Government know what the cost will be?

Likewise, Scotland is a disproportionate user, following a late start, of PFI and PPP type projects. Only as a result of recent changes in accounting standards are these starting to come onto public sector balance sheets. There is little sign that their impact post independence has been analysed.

For capital values at project completion the Scottish share is £5.69bn plus £2.57bn for the newer Non Profit Distributing Projects (NPD) which are currently underway. Again, Scotland has far more than 8.3 per cent of the UK total of £54.2bn., thus implying much heavier per capita servicing costs for this model once outside the UK. Essentially all these models are expensive failures in value terms due to the associated bureaucratic rules and limited competition involved. They are funding models now disliked by voices ranging from the free market Institute of Economic Affairs to the Unison trade union.

NPD has not much changed the problem; schools in Scotland are typically costing 25 per cent more per square metre to build than down south, and still somehow, despite the quasi governmental covenant involved, recent finance structures offer some investors an 11 per cent return. It beats a deposit with the Co-op Bank where some Scottish local authorities unwisely parked spare cash!

Scotland is overweight in such deals, but at least the Barnett formula helps use UK revenues to fund them. An independent Scotland might be forced to sort out the model, but it will be hard to shake down the emerging liabilities.

On a smaller, but still worrying scale, are the finances of rail operations north of the Border. We love our trains, but they will have to be paid for.

Post independence, it is envisaged that the Office of Rail Regulation and Network Rail will continue to operate in Scotland. The newly independent nation would contribute ongoing costs of the attributable network and, somewhat cheekily, will demand a fee for any Scottish underwriting of historic debt.

This is all problematic. Network Rail's accumulated OBS deficit is now a staggering £30 billion, since the tracks cost £4bn-£8bn in subsidy annually. Our glorious but straggling geography means we have some of the least economic lines in the UK, and thus Scotland accounts for 15 per cent of the UK's route miles. So there would be a question of funding (implied formula) £4.5bn of accumulated losses and £600m in annual subsidy going forward. Taking all train subsidies, including the £290m paid annually to First ScotRail, Transport Scotland has revealed that only 26 per cent of the rail operation is funded at the farebox: a £5 ticket on average has around a £15 subsidy, compared to a £4 bung across the UK for that typical spend of a fiver.

Bad as the financial arithmetic of rail will turn out to be for the proud new nation, the operational issues could be worse. If there is no agreement on Scotland assuming these legitimate claims (for Scotland's network has certainly been supported by a significant proportion of that historic OBS debt) then we have the question of whether the employees of Network Rail will actually run services in Scotland; it appears that the employees of Network Rail are not under contracts to a conveniently Scottish entity. They are paid for and directed by a UK private company.

As in so many areas of the independence debate, complex negotiations are needed to ensure transition: many billions are at stake; and there is no recent precedent for just how we disaggregate an integrated asset like rail, or split up and/or fund pensions under new rules.

Off balance sheet these liabilities may be, but in economic terms they are full-on consumers of public cash: a billion here, a billion there – real money. Independence may be an idea whose time has come: but its full financial consequences? These consequences have yet to arrive in terms of public discourse. Bring them on!

Salmond's Stamp Tax on Scottish business

Murdo Fraser
5 April 2014

THE DESCRIPTION "written on the back of a fag packet" is one which is often bandied around in the world of politics to describe policy ideas which are floated without the detailed implications being considered before they are announced.

In the recent constitutional debate around Scottish independence, it is not surprising to see opposition parties regularly using these words to describe SNP proposals for a post-independent Scotland. Sometimes, the description is justified. The perfect example of one such case is in relation to the SNP's plans for the Royal Mail in the event of a Yes vote in the independence referendum.

It was back in September that, in response to the announced privatisation of part of the Royal Mail by the UK Government, the First Minister Alex Salmond announced that in the event of independence the Royal Mail in Scotland would be renationalised. This came as a surprise to many, not least the SNP Finance Secretary, John Swinney. Asked in a BBC Scotland TV debate whether the service would be renationalised, he was unable to give a clear answer as to what the SNP's plans were in the event of independence.

It was only the following day, at First Minster's Questions, that Alex Salmond announced something quite different. In response to a question from my Conservative colleague Gavin Brown MSP, he was quite categorical that an independent Scottish government would "bring the Royal Mail...back into public ownership". The detail of the questioning is quite important here. The First Minster had already been asked by two previous questioners what his plans were, and had declined to be definitive. It was only in response to a third, pointed, and effective, question by Gavin Brown, that he gave a straight answer.

Now it is reasonable to assume that had this been clear SNP policy, Alex Salmond would have been forthcoming at the first opportunity. By holding back until he was pressed on the subject, it certainly looks like this was an answer made up on the hoof, coming as a great surprise both to Mr Swinney and to all his Cabinet colleagues.

This seems rather confirmed by the detail of what has happened since September. We are still no clearer as to the process by which the Royal Mail would be brought back into public ownership in Scotland. The Royal Mail is now, of course, a UK headquartered private company. Even if it wanted to, there is no legal mechanism available to the Scottish Government post independence to nationalise it. The best it can do is negotiate with the Royal Mail in an attempt to purchase its assets in Scotland, and use them as a basis for a new Scottish postal service.

Nor do we know at what price the postal service could be purchased. And we are no clearer as to timescales for this whole process.

It seems to me that the question of ownership of Royal Mail is less important than the question of the service it provides. Despite all the warnings we heard last year, I have yet to see the slightest evidence that there has been a deterioration of service since privatisation. If anything, the opposite has been the case.

What matters to Scottish businesses, particularly those using the postal service and trading cross-border, is the maintenance of the Universal Service Obligation ("USO"). The USO is now enshrined in statute by the UK Parliament, and requires the Royal Mail to ensure a single flat charge for delivering letters across the United Kingdom, regardless of geography. So even businesses and individuals living in the remotest parts of the country will pay no more for a stamp than those living in Edinburgh or London.

The maintenance of the USO is vital to Scottish businesses. It only exists because of an act of the UK Parliament. Dissolve the UK; break up the Royal Mail into two companies (one serving Scotland, and one the rest of the UK); and the USO disappears, as sure as night follows day.

The problem here, as the Chairman of the Institute of Directors in Scotland, Ian McKay (himself a former senior executive at Royal Mail) told Holyrood's Economy, Energy and Tourism Committee on Wednesday, is that the costs of delivering the mail in Scotland are of necessity higher than they are south of the Border. Being integrated into a single UK postal service means cheaper stamps in Scotland. Breaking up the Royal Mail means, inevitably, it will cost more.

So the Scottish Government either has to increase the public subsidy to the Royal Mail, at a time when already it will have to deal with a larger budget deficit than the UK as a whole, or postal charges will have to go up. And that will mean effectively a new tax, a "Salmond Stamp Tax" hitting Scottish consumers and Scottish businesses.

In a series of Parliamentary Questions lodged last week, I tried to ascertain from the SNP government what assessment they had made of additional costs to businesses of a separate postal service in an independent Scotland and with no UK-wide USO. The reply from John Swinney was short and stark: "On independence, stamp prices will be the same as they are at the time in the rest of the UK. A Scottish postal service in public ownership would not need to generate profits for shareholders and so should be in a better position to ensure that postal prices and deliveries meet Scotland's needs. This applies to sending post and parcels within Scotland, to the rest of the UK and to other countries".

So, absolutely no assurance that postal prices will not increase post independence. And no serious attempt by the Scottish Government to address what is a serious issue for business across the country.

On this subject, as on so many others, the lack of detail from a Government trying to persuade us to vote for an independent country is astonishing. Little wonder that Scotland's business organisations keep telling us that their members are highly sceptical about the leap in the dark that Scottish independence represents.

There is a very simple way to avoid Salmond's stamp tax, and that is to vote No in September's referendum. If the SNP think this is scaremongering, then they need to start coming up with some proper answers, and fast.

How a 'debt dump' would lead straight to austerity

Bill Jamieson
15 April 2014

WHEN Scotland's First Minister Alex Salmond first suggested that an independent Scotland might not honour its share of UK public debt it was one of those statements I had to read twice because I couldn't quite believe it the first time.

It seemed, amongst other considerations, such a spectacular own goal. Who would wish to lend to an independent Scotland that began life repudiating its share of debt obligations? In one careless remark Alex Salmond had just raised the cost of borrowing by an independent Scotland several insouciant notches. Perhaps he was just having a bad hair day. But the remark, far from being "corrected" has since been repeated. If Scotland did not get to share the "asset" of the UK pound, it would review its share of the UK liabilities – debt being the largest.

Others have joined in and embellished this view, describing it as "Westminster's debt", incurred by imprudent, spendthrift London governments. But Scotland has long been a recipient of such spending. Indeed, not once do I recall the SNP ever urging that part of the annual Barnet Formula settlement be set aside for debt reduction. In fact, on almost every Budget Day occasion, the SNP has bayed for more.

This paradox notwithstanding, the threat to play politics with debt has been put on the table. And this week, the Centre for Public Policy for Regions (CPPR), a think tank not normally associated with pro-SNP views, published a paper which gave the debt repudiation option a dark credibility.

It set out figures showing how dumping a share of the UK's debt would be worth twice as much to an independent Scotland as North Sea oil. According to the report, the £5.5 billion improvement seen in Scotland's 2016-17 fiscal balance through not having to service existing debt was worth twice as much as the contribution from North Sea tax revenues in that year (put at £2.7 billion, using a geographic share of the latest forecasts from the Office of Budget Responsibility).

This, it said, would improve the nation's fiscal balance from an otherwise poor outlook.

Well, of course it would. The fiscal balances of countries across the world would be transformed if only debt could be dumped!

Lest you thought that by now we have wandered deep into an *Alice in Wonderland* world, Scottish ministers immediately leapt onto the report, saying that it demonstrated Scotland's strong position in the event of a referendum "Yes'" vote. Finance Secretary John Swinney said, "This report shows exactly how strong a hand Scotland will have in negotiations following a vote for independence, and also shows exactly why it will be in the overwhelming economic interests of the rest of the UK to negotiate fairly and openly."

The more negative features of John McLaren's report, pointed out that the Scottish government's "flawed" threat to dump the debt if an independent Scotland could not share the pound under a currency union with the rest of the UK – could lead to cross-border acrimony and disturb international markets, leading to "punitive" borrowing costs.

"Any benefit arising to an independent Scotland from starting with zero historic debt would be heavily influenced by whether this was achieved via amicable negotiations or through Scotland's refusal to accept what the remainder of the UK consider to be an appropriate share."

Never mind. This, for the Nationalists, shows how strong Scotland's negotiating hand is on the issue of currency. Scotland could bluster and bully the rest of the UK into an agreement over sharing the currency – if not, rUK would have to pick up Scotland's debt share. It's hardly a blandishment likely to engender much support for the SNP's position. More likely, it would fuel intense bitterness and division.

However, even if the anger of rUK could be overcome, an independent Scotland free of debt would have at the least a major perception problem.

Once you have politicised debt obligations in this way – choosing to honour one type of debt but refusing to honour another – external lenders would need some persuading to subscribe to any future Scottish debt issue. A country that does this once struggles to shake off a perception that it would do so again.

Debt defaults are rather more common than generally realised. Formally speaking, a sovereign default is the failure or refusal of the government of a sovereign state to pay back its debt in full. It may be accompanied by a formal declaration of a government not to pay (repudiation) or only partially pay its debts (due receivables), or the *de facto cessation* of due payments.

Venezuela has defaulted 11 times, Mexico nine times, Ecuador and El Salvador eight times. They are less common in Europe – though Spain has defaulted on nine occasions, Greece has registered seven – some lasting for long periods, and Austria Hungary six times.

Some economists have argued that, in the case of acute insolvency crises, it can be advisable for regulators and supranational lenders to pre-emptively engineer the orderly restructuring of a nation's public debt – also called "orderly default" or "controlled default.

So, a 'debt dump' need not be catastrophic and certainly not the end of the world for an independent Scotland. And in the last analysis if there was a problem in securing further loans it could always call on the International Monetary Fund. The IMF often assists countries which have difficulties in raising funds in international debt markets.

However, it does have a habit of making its loans conditional on austerity measures within the country, such as tax increases or reductions in public sector jobs and services.

Public sector spending cuts? Austerity measures? Loss of services? Isn't all this exactly what the independence prospectus was intended to spare us?

Debt repudiation is an explosive weapon in cross-border negotiations. It is liable to blow back with spectacular ferocity on those who resort to it, for there are few faster ways to lose friends and torch your economy. Scottish government ministers must take care: burnt fingers would be the least of their problems when they play politics with debt.

The foreign language of xenophobia

Stuart Winton
22 April 2014

MY PREVIOUS ThinkScotland article outlined[1] the inconsistent approach of mainstream Yes campaign thinking to the matter of pooling or ceding sovereignty. From that perspective decisions made in London are *unquestionably bad* for Scotland, whereas power wielded by Brussels is *inherently good* and afforded little in the way of debate, never mind critique.

The UK/EU comparison also demonstrates something of a dichotomy when it comes to language. And in that regard it's worth noting that in contemporary discourse choice of words can be employed to inflame and demonise, even attracting the attention of the criminal law in extreme cases.

But, more mundanely, it's commonplace to label opponents of the EU in terms like 'Europhobe' or the slightly stronger 'xenophobe'. Indeed, one correspondent[2] to *The Scotsman* alluded that opposition to the EU was inherently racist (while on other occasions ironically demonstrating a rather reverential attitude towards Margaret Thatcher). Commentator Ruth Wishart described[3] UKIP members as 'headbangers' and the Tories as having an 'obsessive compulsive disorder' against the EU. By the

243

same token, but in an ostensibly more sober and objective environment, a recent *Sunday Herald* newspiece casually described UKIP as an anti-EU party.

However, imagine the reaction if a news article had described the SNP as an anti-UK party. Or Yes campaigners were described as Anglophobes, or as headbangers having an 'obsessive compulsive disorder' regarding the UK. But, as a supporter of independence for Scotland, Ruth Wishart should surely be labelled in such terms to be consistent with her own rhetoric. Likewise Yes supporter Lesley Riddoch, who wrote[4] in terms of 'Europhobic English'. Does that make Yes campaigners *Anglophobic Scots*?

A related point is that those who, for example, demonstrate a holier-than-thou approach to the slightest criticism of a nation or ethnic group (say), can themselves talk pejoratively in such matters when it suits. For example, Gordon MacIntyre-Kemp of pro-Yes group Business for Scotland wrote[5], in the context of EU member states: "It could even be described as xenophobic to suggest that countries that enter into integrated common markets and/or shared currency agreements are not truly independent."

Which would mean, for example, that Mark Carney, the Canadian governor of the Bank of England who said that an independent Scotland entering into a currency union with the continuing UK would entail a loss of sovereignty, is a xenophobe.

Moreover, contrast Mr MacIntyre-Kemp's sanctimony with a statement made by Ivan McKee, another Business for Scotland representative. When BP chief executive Bob Dudley warned of the 'uncertainties' surrounding the question of independence and expressed support for the UK, Mr McKee said[6]: "For an American to come out and say Great Britain is great with that kind of British nationalist perspective is interesting, sitting as he is in a London bubble for sure."

So it seems that in the world of Business for Scotland it's xenophobic to suggest that EU membership entails some ceding of sovereignty, while it's OK to talk pejoratively in terms of an "American", a "British nationalist" and a "London bubble".

Of course, the latter slur is interesting, because Yes campaigners generally avoid talking negatively in terms of England *per se* – presumably to avoid accusations of Anglophobia – and instead the targets are usually more specific. For example, 'Westminster', 'Tories' and the 'dark star' of London are favourite slurs from even the most senior SNP politicians, conveniently sidestepping the fact that such institutions are an integral part of England (or the UK) as a nation.

But often the veil slips, and a more directly derogatory use of the E-word is employed. For example, former SNP leader Gordon Wilson referred[7] to the "cancer" of London and the south east of England, only narrowly avoiding labelling the English as a whole. More specifically, Yes supporter and man of the common people Sir George Mathewson complained[8] of "snooty English" people "coming up and telling us how things are going to be". More recently, SNP MP Stewart Hosie expressed[9] similar sentiments on BBC's *Question Time*, saying: "Can we stop having English Tory MPs turning up in Edinburgh to bully the Scots and to poison the relationships between Scotland and England."

By the same token, a recent piece by a *Herald* features writer described[10] how an "English toff" prime minister, a cabinet of "English Tory millionaires" and "the toxic taint of English Toryism" have helped maintain Scots' sense of alienation.

Last year Robin McAlpine of the Jimmy Reid Foundation opined[11]: "The simple fact is that there is no term, no phraseology, no usage of any description that Scots use to denigrate the English."

That view is surely more than a tad naïve, however. Depending on context, it's surely the case that the term 'English' *per se* is used in a derogatory fashion, as the relatively benign examples used here surely demonstrate.

So despite Yes protestations, it's reasonably self-evident that the independence campaign is not just rationalised in terms of opposition to London, Westminster, Toryism, poshness, millionaires etc, since there's more than a hint that being English *per se* is the problem. Which, of course, the SNP has to an extent been successful in challenging in terms of reorienting the movement from more traditional 'ethnic' nationalism to the more modern 'civic' variety. But in which endeavour it has demonstrably not been wholly successful, despite normally avoiding the use of the E-word, and in spite of the self-righteousness normally evident when opponents talk critically in relation to the likes of the EU.

The double standard of the Yes campaigners and the left more generally in the use of such language was amusingly demonstrated by Edinburgh Green councillor Chas Booth, who said on TV: "In many respects, the rise of UKIP, which is effectively an anti-EU, anti-immigrant party in England, for many Scots that makes them look at England and say well actually this is becoming an increasingly foreign country to us, we don't recognise this xenophobia, this anti-foreigner approach by UKIP."

Clearly, disliking 'foreign' countries is only xenophobic when it suits!

1 http://www.thinkscotland.org/thinkpolitics/articles.html?read_full=12493
2 http://www.scotsman.com/news/opinion/letters/class-interests-still-motivate-the-tories-1-2465437
3 http://bellacaledonia.org.uk/2013/01/23/euve-been-framed/
4 http://www.lesleyriddoch.co.uk/2012/12/europe-scotland-all-shook-up.html
5 http://www.businessforscotland.co.uk/economic-policy-in-an-independent-scotland/
6 http://www.youtube.com/watch?v=I9lOyA_3p44
7 http://www.telegraph.co.uk/news/uknews/scotland/10240802/Former-SNP-leader-tells-Alex-Salmond-Attack-the-English-southern-cancer-to-win-referendum.html

8 http://www.newsnetscotland.com/index.php/referendum/7274-financial-giant-very-angry-at-distortion-of-independence-facts

9 http://ahdinnaeken.wordpress.com/2014/02/24/why-indyref-is-a-bore-in-seven-quotes/

10 http://www.heraldscotland.com/comment/columnists/a-yes-vote-could-be-making-of-the-right-wing-in-scotland.23240613

11 http://www.heraldscotland.com/comment/columnists/a-yes-vote-could-be-making-of-the-right-wing-in-scotland.23240613